INDUSTRY
IN POLAND
STRUCTURAL
ADJUSTMENT ISSUES
AND
POLICY OPTIONS

ORGANISATION FOR ECONOMIC CO-OPERATION AND DEVELOPMENT
CENTRE FOR CO-OPERATION WITH THE EUROPEAN ECONOMIES IN TRANSITION

ORGANISATION FOR ECONOMIC CO-OPERATION AND DEVELOPMENT

Pursuant to Article 1 of the Convention signed in Paris on 14th December 1960, and which came into force on 30th September 1961, the Organisation for Economic Co-operation and Development (OECD) shall promote policies designed:

— to achieve the highest sustainable economic growth and employment and a rising standard of living in Member countries, while maintaining financial stability, and thus to contribute to the development of the world economy;

— to contribute to sound economic expansion in Member as well as non-member countries in the process of economic development; and

— to contribute to the expansion of world trade on a multilateral, non-discriminatory basis in accordance with international obligations.

The original Member countries of the OECD are Austria, Belgium, Canada, Denmark, France, Germany, Greece, Iceland, Ireland, Italy, Luxembourg, the Netherlands, Norway, Portugal, Spain, Sweden, Switzerland, Turkey, the United Kingdom and the United States. The following countries became Members subsequently through accession at the dates indicated hereafter: Japan (28th April 1964), Finland (28th January 1969), Australia (7th June 1971) and New Zealand (29th May 1973). The Commission of the European Communities takes part in the work of the OECD (Article 13 of the OECD Convention).

The Czech and Slovak Federal Republic, Hungary and Poland participate in the OECD Programme "Partners in Transition", which is managed by the Centre for Co-operation with European Economies in Transition.

Publié en français sous le titre :

L'INDUSTRIE EN POLOGNE :
PROBLÈMES ET POLITIQUES D'ADAPTATION STRUCTURELLE

Foreword

The Center for Co-operation with European Economies in Transition (CCEET), which was created in March 1990, is a focal point for co-operation between the OECD and Central and Eastern European countries. Its major responsibility is to design and manage a programme of policy advice and technical assistance which puts the expertise of the Secretariat and Member countries at the disposal of countries engaged in economic reform.

The programme "Partners in Transition" was launched in 1991 for the purpose of providing more focused assistance to the three countries (Hungary, the Czech and Slovak Federative Republic and Poland) that are more advanced in introducing market-oriented reforms and desire to become Members of OECD.

In the context of this programme, which is managed by the CCEET, the OECD Industry Committee undertook an examination of the problems of industrial restructuring in Poland with the aim of helping the Polish Government define the orientations of its policy to promote industrial adjustment to the new market conditions. This examination took place on 16 June 1992 in Warsaw at the invitation of the Polish Ministry of Industry and Commerce.

The present report, which served as a basis for these discussions, has been prepared by Jean Guinet, from the OECD Directorate for Science, Technology and Industry, and Alice Amsden, from the Massachusetts Institute of Technology, consultant. This report has also benefitted from extensive comments and revisions by several OECD departments and the CCEET. It is based on information gathered in close co-operation with the Polish Ministry of Industry and Trade and with Promasz, a Polish consulting firm.

It is published on the responsibility of the Secretary-General of the OECD.

Salvatore Zecchini

Assistant Secretary-General
Director of the CCEET

Publications in the CCEET Series

Industrial Policy in OECD Countries -- Annual Review 1992
October 1992 Format 16X23 200 pages
(70 92 05 1) ISBN 92-64-13765-3   FF150   £21.00   US$37.00   DM61

Short-Term Economic Statistics -- Central and Eastern Europe
January 1992 (Bilingual) Format 16X23 390 pages
(14 92 01 3) ISBN 92-64-03523-0   FF 120   £ 16.00   US$ 32.00   DM 48

The Transition to a Market Economy: Volume 1 -- The Broad Issues.
Volume 2 -- Special Issues (CCEET)
January 1992   (Bilingual) Format 16X23 750 pages
(14 91 06 3) ISBN 92-64-03520-6   FF300   £42.00   US$72.00   DM12
Two volumes not sold separately

OECD Economic Surveys/CCEET. 1991-1992 Series:
Poland
July 1992 Format 16X23 202 pages
(09 92 03 1) ISBN 92-64-13723-8   FF90   £13.00   US$20.00   DM37

Hungary
August 1991 Format 16X23 202 pages
(09 92 01 1) ISBN 92-64-13554-5   FF90   £13.00   US$20.00   DM37

Czech and Slovak Federal Republic
December 1991 Format 16X23 148 pages
(09 92 02 1) ISBN 92-64-13607-X   FF90   £13.00   US$20.00   DM37

Price for the three surveys: Hungary, Poland, Czech and Slovak Federal Republic
                               FF230   £32.00   US$52.00   DM95

Prices charged at the OECD Bookshop.
THE OECD CATALOGUE OF PUBLICATIONS and supplements will be sent free of charge
on request addressed either to the OECD Publications Service or to the Distributor in your country.

Table of contents

Maps

Tables

Text

Charts

Introduction

For over two years, Poland has been undergoing radical economic change. To establish a market economy is a vast undertaking in terms of the number, range and importance of the reforms to be carried out. These reforms affect practically every aspect of the institutional and legal system governing the economy. They mean the removal of many components of the previous system, the provision of new institutions, and the creation *ex nihilo* of the legal infrastructure necessary to the operation of a market economy. They must be underpinned by macroeconomic stabilisation measures that will create conditions conducive to structural changes, particularly by making these conditions less dependent on the shock waves inevitably caused by the collapse of the former structures and the sudden liberalisation of markets.

In the face of this tremendous task, the Polish authorities have shown great determination in maintaining the course they set in late 1989. They deserve credit both for their outstanding efforts and for some remarkable results. As the recent *OECD Economic Survey on Poland[1]* stressed, economic history gives no other example of such accomplishments in so short a time. Poland has made many radical and irreversible changes in the economic system, which have given rise to already perceptible positive effects, such as the disappearance of shortages and the rapid development of private enterprise.

Nevertheless, the way ahead is long and strewn with obstacles. Some difficulties were foreseen. The reform's backers foresaw that the transition phase would include a period of output decline caused by the process of macroeconomic stabilisation and the inevitabe delay in adjusting supply to the new market-oriented incentive structure. The most optimistic among them however expected that the effects of this "recession", particularly on the confidence of citizens and foreign investors, would be limited, and that the difficult spell would be short-lived and could be weathered without altering course.

The actual outcome has obviously not met the highest expectations and has probably surprised even the most cautious observers. The drop in national income has been sharper and lasted longer than was anticipated; and the associated rise in adjustment costs, particularly in terms of unemployment, has tended to overshadow the positive developments. Even if the overall level of consumption has been broadly maintained in the last two years, and the development of the "grey" market has made life less difficult in this respect, many households have suffered from the erosion of their purchasing power and are haunted by the fear of unemployment. These fears are particularly widespread in the regions and localities where the most hard-hit industries are concentrated.

The weakening of public support for the reform programme, as indicated by the pre-election turbulences, is one of the most disturbing aspects of recent developments. Yet the public appears to be still generally convinced that there is no real alternative to the economic strategy adopted, but they are urging the government to consider every means of bringing the crisis more quickly to an end and finding a way to make up for lost ground and enter a phase of sustained growth.

The government formed after the last election has stated that it does not intend to change in any basic way the reform strategy implemented since early 1990, but it does intend to halt the decline in GDP and speed up the restructuring of microeconomic structures in 1992. The Polish authorities remain convinced that Poland's conversion to a market economy is a long-term operation that requires perseverance and continuity in implementing the reforms already under way. However, in response to social unrest, they are driven by a sense of urgency. They are looking for ways and means to speed up the recovery without running the risk of compromising the results achieved and slowing down or distorting the necessary structural changes.

Since an expansionist macroeconomic policy has been ruled out as ineffective and hazardous, the government will have to fine-tune existing macroeconomic measures and improve structural policies. Industrial policy, in the widest sense, is an important component of such policies; the object of this report, undertaken as part of the "Partners in Transition programme", is to see how it can best contribute to achieving Poland's economic objectives.

The part to be played by industrial policy in Poland today cannot be simply deduced from the experience of market economies. The specific characteristics of the transition period must be taken into account. The particularities of the incubation phase in major reforms, the boldness of the adopted approach, the magnitude of the planned changes, and the lack of historical or theoretical references to assess the progress made and appreciate the nature of the obstacles encountered, are factors that must not be overlooked in an analysis of Poland's situation.

The political and economic turning point of 1989 was preceded by a long period of economic stagnation and social unrest that forced the authorities to take a series of steps to amend the planned economy system. The effects of the unsuccessful expansion policy based on the import of capital equipment in the 1970's and the rise of an organised opposition led by the trade unions in the 1980's forced them to seek new ways to improve economic performance. They introduced various reforms that were generally intended to decentralise investment decisions, and some company management powers were officially transferred to the workers' councils. Although these reforms did not achieve their objectives, they did speed up the dissolution of the central planning system, without however leading to the emergence of an alternative system. The result was that in 1989 Poland could be described as having "neither plan nor market". The State had in fact abandoned its powers as a shareholder in firms and kept only its authority to intervene financially (subsidies) and on the regulatory side (control of prices and foreign trade). The full effects of its surrender of shareholder power on the motivation of managers only appeared when the State gave up the remainder of its prerogatives at the start of 1990. It is impossible to understand the limitations on the options for privatisation policy (the fact that workers' councils have been given a *veto* right) and for industrial restructuring policy (the political resistance in certain worker strongholds) without an awareness of the historical conditions that led to the legalisation of the role of workers' councils by the former regime and to the political endorsement (and therefore activation) of the councils' power by the democratic movement.

The history of ineffective reforms in the 1970s and 1980s probably influenced the Polish government's decision in late 1989 to opt for switching suddenly rather than gradually to a market economy. The most original and daring aspect of this strategy was to make zloty convertibility the starting point and not the end point of the transformation process. Instead of subordinating price and trade liberalisation to progress in systemic reforms, the inertia of existing structures would be overcome by the initial shock of liberalisation and stabilization. This strategy has generally paid off, but its originality prevented foreseeing all its consequences, and therefore Poland experienced a number of setbacks. It must be kept in mind that this approach to structural reform means not only strict adherence to a strategic course, but also constant adaptation to hazards and to unexpected developments.

A "clean break" strategy requires radical changes in the economic ground rules, notably the abrupt introduction of a competitive discipline based on stringent world market criteria. It has the merit of sharply revealing the immense need for an adjustment of attitudes and microeconomic structures. It also creates powerful incentives to meet this need, owing to the pressures of irreversibility it causes. But the suddenness and magnitude of this need for adjustment raise three questions. Are the adjustment pressures passed on without undue distortion to the different groups of economic actors? Are these actors sufficiently motivated to react to these pressures in the right way? Are they able to do so?

— When a number of firms still hold dominant positions in their markets, there is a serious possibility that the pressures will be diverted.

— There is also a risk of undesirable reactions to adjustment pressures, owing to the current weakness of management principles in state-owned firms.

— Actual adjustment capabilities are limited by two factors. First, access to funds is restricted due to the need for macroeconomic stabilisation, the indebtedness of most firms and the financial vulnerability of banks. Second, it is easier to introduce quickly the stringent rules of the market economy than the components that normally accompany them — an efficient financial system, a good infrastructure for technology diffusion, a well developed labour market, etc. — so that a general balance can be struck between incentives and capabilities.

A temporary imbalance is probably inevitable in the early days of the transition process. A lasting imbalance would be detrimental to Poland, for it would mean adjustment at a lower level, and therefore a reduction of the stock of useful capital and production potential, with no increase in medium-term growth potential.

The Polish government cannot turn to any known formulae to ensure the right mix between pressures and incentives, between the carrot and the stick. It is facing unprecedented problems. The transition to a market economy raises issues very different, for example, from those of the period of economic reconstruction in Western Europe or Japan after the second World War. Both the national and world economic contexts have changed. Poland does not have to replace, in an existing market framework, a capital stock that has been physically destroyed; it has to adapt an existing industrial structure to the demands of a market environment that it must set up from scratch. In addition, it has to do so at a time of globalisation of markets and business strategy and of very rapid technological change.

Neither is Poland's case really comparable with that of industrialising countries, even if something can probably be learnt from some of them, particularly the most dynamic in South-East Asia. In many respects Poland is highly developed, but within a system that has failed. It is restructuring rather than industrialising. Finally Poland's case does not fit completely into the conceptual schemes that are used to ground the structural adjustment policies of OECD countries. None of these frameworks address market imperfections on such a massive scale as those now seen in the Polish economy. The Polish authorities must synthesize the experience of OECD and industrialising countries, while at the same time remaining continually prepared to adapt both strategies and instruments to the unfolding experience.

For example, "recession" is a common economic concept which must be used carefully. Poland is not at present in a recession in the usual meaning of the word. The very marked and continuous decline in economic activity that has been observed in the last two years is connected with the current process of structural change. It does not come under the conventional pattern of economic fluctuations to which corrective macroeconomic measures might be applicable. It mainly indicates that the difficulties of adjusting supply structures to the demands of emerging market forces are so far having a greater impact on overall economic output than has the progress made in exploiting new opportunities (e.g. rapid growth of the private sector) or in improving the macroeconomic basis (e.g. hyperinflation brought under control and credibility of the zloty ensured). There are many reasons why the adjustment of productive structures is causing such difficulties.

— The first is the varying time span, which sometimes cannot be reduced, for implementing systemic reforms. Some reforms require only a few months to take full effect, while others take years. The market environment is thus deprived for a long time of certain vital components.

— The second reason is the natural inertia of existing structures. Major changes in production processes and product ranges cannot be made from one day to the next, especially when they require completely overhauling the existing capital stock. Capital-intensive activities are particularly affected. The fact that capital is indi-

15

visible causes threshold effects in these activities, so that the inadequacy of financial resources may not only slow the adjustment process but actually prevent its start.

— The third reason is the existence of factors that distort incentives for firms. Two are of particular importance. First, the penalties for poor management, particularly bankruptcy, lack credibility. Second, those who have management powers in the state sector are usually not sufficiently interested in defending the market value of firms; management strategy is often directed less at maximising the discounted value of future profits than at maximising variable costs, namely wages.

— Finally, the first two years of transition in Poland did not take place in a favourable international environment. Western economies have not been buoyant and export markets in which Polish producers had specialised have collapsed. Markets in Lybia and Iraq have been lost and, above all, the sudden disappearance of many markets in the ex-CMEA (Council of Mutual Economic Assistance) countries, compounded by a sudden rise in prices for energy imports from the ex-USSR, has added to the effects of the internal obstacles to structural adjustment.

Macroeconomic circumstances (tight money and budget difficulties) act as a lense that focuses the beam from all these factors. Industry is probably most affected, if only because it has the greatest number and proportion of state firms. The blockage of adjustment mechanisms is reflected in a very serious deterioration in the situation of many industrial firms. The expedients which they are tempted to use in order to survive (e.g. inter-company credit or accumulating loans from the banking system or the State) simply spread the disease, which is now indiscriminately threatening non-viable and potentially viable firms. In its turn, the crisis among state industrial firms has unfavourable repercussions on the possibilities for privatisation and the development potential of private-sector small-and-medium size enterprises engaged in sub-contracting work. It is also undermining the budget situation and the financial system's equilibrium. The risk is that a vicious circle will be formed.

It is because of this risk that the industrial restructuring process is now central in the debate on the transition problem, and that the first order of business for the Polish authorities is to find ways to speed up this process. The object of the present report is to contribute to this reflexion by proposing an interpretation of the nature of current industrial adjustment problems and by assessing the main options for action.

Chapter 1

The current situation

I.   Recent trends

Since Poland introduced its transformation programme in the beginning of 1990, it has experienced sharp declines in per capita income (GDP fell by 12 per cent in 1990, and by 7 per cent in 1991) and the industrial output of state-owned firms (in 1991 it was only two-thirds of its 1989 level). As Chart 1 indicates, the fall in real GDP in Poland over 1990-1991 was greater than in the other two "Partners in Transition" (PIT) countries, the CSFR and Hungary, yet in 1991 this trend was showings signs of levelling off in Poland while the decline continued in the CSFR and Hungary, matching or exceeding that in Poland. The small private sector, principally in services, has boomed. Trade with the OECD area has also flourished, although Poland experienced a negative trade balance in the first half of 1991. The rate of inflation has fallen from 550 per cent in 1990 to about 65 per cent in 1991, per annum, but unemployement has risen to about 12 per cent.

This chapter reviews recent macroeconomic and industrial trends in Poland. It then discusses Poland's progress thus far on structural reforms.

A. *The macroeconomic context*

Poland has undertaken its transformation into a market economy amidst a tight external constraint. Its high foreign debt, incurred under central planning, has made further foreign borrowing to finance re-industrialisation difficult. Unless foreign direct investment is to dramatically accelerate, Poland must generate foreign exchange through trade in order to purchase the technology and capital goods it requires to restructure.

Exports to and imports from countries outside the former CMEA bloc have increased sharply. However, the steep decline in exports to former CMEA countries has offset the sharp increase in exports to the rest of the world, resulting in a flat aggregate growth rate in exports since 1990.

17

Chart 1. MAJOR ECONOMIC TRENDS
IN CENTRAL AND EASTERN EUROPE

Main indications

	Poland			CSFR			Hungary		
	1989	1990	1991*	1989	1990	1991*	1989	1990	1991*
Real GDP [1], % change [2]	0.5	-12	-7	1	-1.1	-12	-0.2	-5	-7
Industrial output, % change [2]	-0.5	-24.2	-11.8	1	-3.7	-4.5	-1	-10	-12
Exports, $ bn	15.6	18.6	18.6	14.3	13.5	13.7	10.9	10.8	11.4
Imports, $ bn	17.4	14.7	18.8	17.1	19	16.5	12.4	12.6	11.3
Inflation rates, %	251	585	70	1.4	10	55	17	29	38
Unemployment rates, %	0.3	6.1	12	0	1	7.5	0.5	1.7	8
Trade balance, $ bn	-1.8	3.8	-0.2	-2.8	-5.5	-2.8	-1.5	-1.8	-0.1
Exchange rate per $	1 446	9 500	10 730[3]	15	18.2	29	59.1	63.2	75

* Estimates

1 . GDP for Poland and Hungary ; Net Material Product for the CSFR.
2. Over previous year.
3. Free market rate ; official rate : 10500.

Source : OECD.

An indicative recovery scenario
in Central and Eastern Europe

GDP per person, 1989 dollars

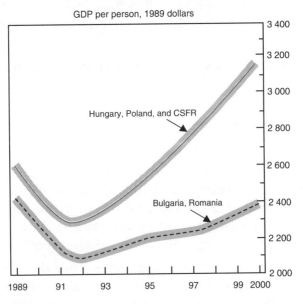

Source: World Bank.

18

Imports jumped from $14.7 billion in 1990 to almost $19 billion a year later. Their share in domestic absorption rose from 14.6 per cent in 1989 to 24.9 per cent in 1991. The share of consumer goods rose steeply, and both light industry and food industry doubled their import shares. In 1991, the private sector accounted for 22 per cent of exports and 50 per cent of imports. In the first half of 1991, total export growth slowed from 24.5 per cent to 8.7 per cent in the second half (compared to the same period of the previous year).

Poland's rate of exchange of zlotys per dollar depreciated from 1 446 in 1989 to 9 500 in 1990 to 10 500 in 1991, but because of inflation, the real exchange rate in 1991 appreciated sharply. The index of Ecus and dollars per zloty rose from roughly 100 at the beginning of the year to almost 140 at the end.

The environment in which Poland has had to restructure is also marked by financial fragility, with an embryonic private banking sector, and an active inter-firm debt market (see Chart 2). At the beginning of 1990, real interest rates were extremely high. They seem to have fallen in the second half of 1990 when inflation accelerated, but throughout most of 1991, with a decline in inflation, they again become strongly positive. Investment fell by 18 per cent in 1990, after been positive in low single digit figures in the late 1980s.

Amidst the uncertainties that accompanied the introduction of a stabilisation package in January 1990, real wages dropped sharply. In the six months between September 1989 and March 1990, they fell by 47.2 per cent. Thereafter, they tended to fluctuate around a declining trend (see Chart 2). These declines overstated a fall in welfare because Polish consumers no longer faced lengthy queues and because they were cushioned by the rapid development of "grey" economy. Yet they also understated a decline in welfare because social services (health care, for example) have also declined.

With a surge in imports, rising real interest rates, and falling real wages, output fell more than was expected. Simultaneously, employment fell — total measured employment was roughly the same in 1990 as in the 1970s — and unemployment rose to over 12 per cent at the end of 1991, especially affecting young people and women, who make up over half the unemployed. In terms of regional distribution, it is thus far highly skewed towards centres of heavy industry and scattered industrial sites. The unemployment rate was believed to have been overstated by the registration of the "voluntary unemployed" — people who had never worked but who registered in order to draw possible unemployment allowances.

Chart 2. **THE MACROECONOMIC CONTEXT**
MAIN INDICATORS

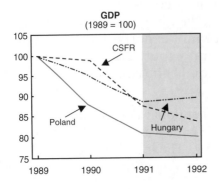

GDP
(1989 = 100)

Unemployment (Right scale %)
Real wages (Jan. 1989 = 100)

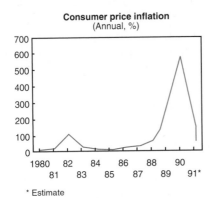

Consumer price inflation
(Annual, %)

* Estimate

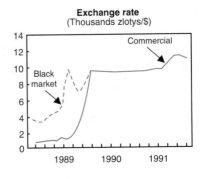

Exchange rate
(Thousands zlotys/$)

Consumer price inflation
(Monthly,%)

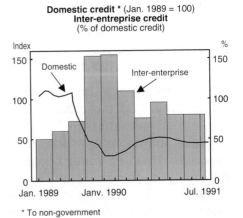

Domestic credit * (Jan. 1989 = 100)
Inter-entreprise credit
(% of domestic credit)

* To non-government

Sources: Various Polish official sources.

Regulations preventing this were tightened after July 1990, and unemployment may have become understated due to the "discouraged worker effect", or the failure of workers with few job prospects to register.

Because Polish industry had been overstaffed under central planning, high rates of unemployment were expected to accompany the process of restructuring. Nevertheless, while industrial output in state-owned enterprises in 1990 fell by around 25 per cent (Chart 3), these enterprises reduced employment by only around 14 per cent. Consequently, productivity fell sharply. The relatively small share of unemployment that has been accounted for by mass layoffs suggests the likelihood of even higher rates of unemployment in the future once enterprise restructuring gets underway. In fact, in the first quarter of 1992, there were early signs of an acceleration in employment rationalisation. For the first time since the beginning of the transition, the decrease in employment was greater than that in production (by 9.3 and 8.6 per cent, respectively, compared to the previous year). The government projects that the unemployment rate could reach at least 17 per cent at the end of 1992.

Chart 3. **INDUSTRIAL PRODUCTION**
Dec. 1988 = 100

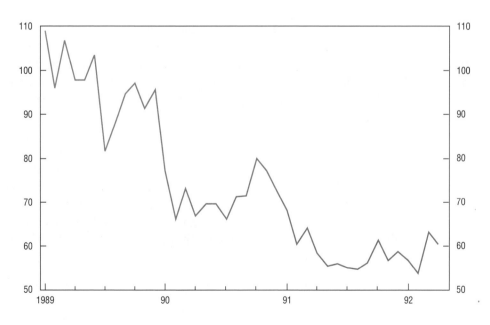

Source: Polish Central Statistical Office.

The macroeconomic situation in Poland remains fragile. A primary objective of stabilization policy has been to reduce inflation, by maintaining tight control over the money supply, balancing the State budget and containing wage increase. Pressures to increase wages without regard to labour productivity remain strong. The budget deficit threatens to increase again as revenues from state-owned enterprises decline and government tax revenues dwindle. Taxes collected from state-owned enterprises accounted for a very large share of State revenues. The profitability of these enterprises, however, has generally plunged into the red. The most recent information indicates an increase in the number of medium and large enterprises registering deficit (see Chart 4).

In mid-1991, the slide of the budget into deficit was not arrested and partly as a result, the IMF programme was temporarily suspended. After the adoption of the 1992 Budget Act which stipulates a limit to the budget deficit equal to 5 per cent of GDP, a return to implementation of the IMF programme is likely. This has led to pressures for further cutbacks in social services and investments in infrastructure and training which might otherwise help restructuring.

B. Recent developments in industry

1. Pressures for change

Since the transition began, Polish industry has been subject to both exogenous and endogenous pressures. One endogenous pressure concerns the dramatic changes in relative prices. Table 1 suggests that the retail price index has tended to rise faster than the wholesale price index, particularly in 1991. This is partly a consequence of the expanding weight of services and imports in the consumption bundle, and the fast increase in the price of services, largely provided by the private sector. Table 1 also indicates a surge in energy prices (see also Table 1.8 in the Annex). The price of metallurgical products (iron and steel and non-ferrous metals) increased almost as much as that of energy in 1990, but in 1991 metallurgical products had the lowest price increase of all industries. Among the industry sectors whose price increases were consistently lowest were light industry (textiles, clothing and leather) and engineering (mechanical and electrical machinery, precision instruments).

In addition to changes in domestic relative prices, Polish industry also faced pressures from the collapse of ex-CMEA trade and a spurt in imports. The collapse of ex-CMEA trade is estimated to have led to a decline in aggregate GNP of 3 per cent, but certain industries were espe-

Chart 4. **RECENT TRENDS IN POLISH INDUSTRY**
MAIN INDICATORS

Industrial production and investment
(1988 = 100)

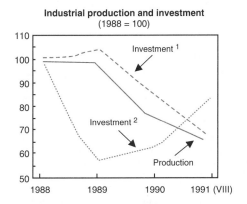

1. Tangible: Gross Fixed Capital Formation
2. Intangible: R&D expenditures as % of sales

Employment and productivity
(1988 = 100)

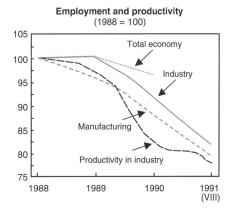

Stocks

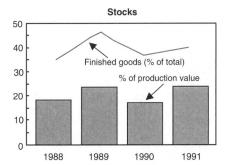

Imports and exports
(1988 = 100)

Exports as % of sales
Imports as % of domestic use

Credit to industry (% of total)
and interest rates [1] (Right scale)

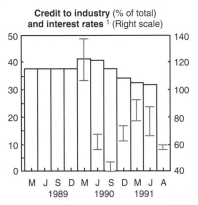

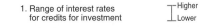

1. Range of interest rates
   for credits for investment

Higher
Lower

Profitability [1]
(%)

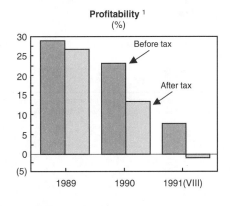

1. Profit as % of total costs

Sources: OECD; Polish Ministry of Industry and Trade (Promasz); other official sources.

Table 1.   Changes in relative prices, 1987-1991[1]

% of overall price index

	1987	1988	1989	1990	1991
CPI / PPI	100.0	100.3	112.5	106.7	122.8
Consumer prices-total	100.0	100.0	100.0	100.0	100.0
Goods	100.0	99.6	103.4	99.6	93.4
Food	100.0	93.3	111.6	110.0	94.2
Services	100.0	102.1	78.7	100.2	137.5
Producer prices-total	100.0	100.0	100.0	100.0	100.0
Energy	100.0	106.5	81.1	116.0	146.5
Coal	100.0	105.6	62.9	87.0	122.6
Fuel	100.0	110.2	95.8	132.5	147.3
Power	100.0	101.6	89.1	132.9	173.5
Metallurgy	100.0	104.8	111.5	136.4	110.2
Iron and steel	100.0	99.7	114.0	136.3	109.2
Non-ferrous metals	100.0	113.4	108.7	137.0	113.6
Engineering	100.0	97.3	94.3	85.3	79.3
Metal products	100.0	97.1	97.7	94.0	84.6
Engineering	100.0	95.5	86.5	77.0	70.7
Precision equipment	100.0	95.3	83.5	60.7	52.8
Transport equipment	100.0	98.1	99.7	98.6	100.8
Electronics	100.0	100.2	100.2	83.7	71.2
Chemicals	100.0	101.5	95.7	102.8	97.7
Mineral products	100.0	97.8	94.2	94.7	92.7
Building materials	100.0	95.9	86.8	90.8	88.9
Glass	100.0	102.4	110.4	106.6	104.0
Earthenware/ceramics	100.0	104.6	122.4	103.4	104.6
Wood and paper	100.0	92.8	98.7	90.1	87.0
Wood	100.0	91.6	98.5	83.3	85.2
Paper	100.0	96.1	100.1	106.3	86.9
Light industry	100.0	98.4	101.9	71.7	66.4
Textiles	100.0	98.7	100.0	74.7	65.9
Clothing	100.0	95.1	93.9	57.4	56.5
Leather	100.0	100.8	115.3	79.4	73.5
Food	100.0	98.5	123.1	107.0	110.1
Other industrial categories	100.0	99.6	88.9	79.1	81.3
Animal feed	100.0	120.0	99.5	67.4	56.3
Printing	100.0	93.9	81.0	73.4	90.5
Miscellaneous	100.0	95.4	89.0	86.2	84.1

1. Including state units, co-operative units and units of political organisations and trade unions.
Source: Polish Central Statistical Office (GUS).

cially hard-hit. As Chart 5 indicates, in 1991 mechanical and electrical engineering industries had both the largest share of exports to ex-CMEA countries (as a percentage of 1988 sales) and the largest export declines. Textiles, leather products, iron and steel, fabricated metals, and wood products also experienced above average falls in ex-CMEA exports.

As for imports, a jump in imports in total domestic absorption, from 14.6 per cent in 1989 to 24.9 per cent in 1991, was reflected in almost all sectors. The sectors whose share of imports in total use roughly doubled were mineral and non-metallic products, wood and paper products, light industry, and processed foods. In almost all industries, the rise in imports in total domestic absorption was greatest between 1990 and 1991. This coincided with a sharp drop in Poland's customs tariffs and the appreciation of the zloty. For all categories, the average tariff rate was 18.3 per cent from January 1989, 5.5 per cent from August 1990, and 18.4 per cent after August 1991.

2. Trends by industrial sector

Chart 5 gives a breakdown by industry for the period 1989 to 1991 (first eight months) of changes in sales, employment, productivity and profitability. The chart on profitability shows that profitability for all industries fell sharply over time. Yet there does not appear to be any simple relationship between sales, productivity, and profitability. For instance, the non-ferrous metals sector had one of the highest profit margin of all sectors in 1991, but experienced one of the steepest declines in sales and productivity. In 1991, price increases in this sector were also among the lowest. Clearly, other factors were influencing profitability. In contrast, the fuel and energy sector had one of the highest rates of price increase but about half of all enterprises in this sector experienced losses in 1990. Generally, profitability measures for broadly-defined industries appear to have a lot of dispersion about the mean. In 1990, for example, in the textile and leather products industries, about one-third of all firms showed losses, and the remaining two-thirds made profits.

Chart 5 indicates that the industries with the "best" sales performance (lowest drop in sales) were the glass, wood, building materials, paper, and processed food industries. These industries also tended to have below average rates of productivity decline. Yet they were not consistently among the top exporters, nor were they all above average in terms of investment.

Obviously the transition is too new to make any definitive statements about industry behaviour. The evidence available suggests, however, that current profitability may not be a good indicator of performance, given the

Chart 5. **RECENT TRENDS IN POLISH INDUSTRY**
MAIN SECTORAL INDICATORS

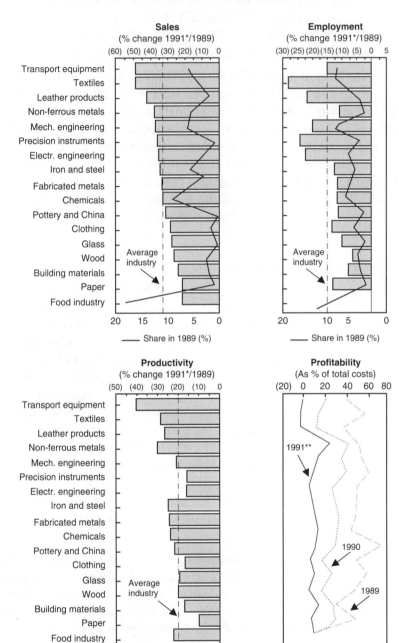

*   First eight months
** First seven months

Source: Polish Ministry of Industry and Trade (Promasz).

Chart 5. RECENT TRENDS IN POLISH INDUSTRY
MAIN SECTORAL INDICATORS (cont'd)
EXPORTS

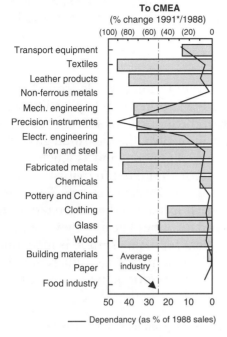

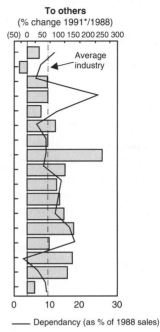

——— Dependancy (as % of 1988 sales)

INVESTMENT

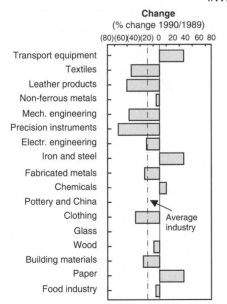

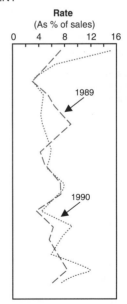

* First six months

Source: Polish Ministry of Industry and Trade (Promasz).

turbulent times and the large number of structural changes all industries are undergoing. Moreover, it may be necessary to extend the analysis from broadly defined industry to single firms in order to make sense of Poland's economic performance, since some firms in an industry appear to be doing well while others are doing poorly.

3. Emerging structural changes

In addition to a spectacular reorientation in trade from the defunct CMEA bloc to the OECD countries, another highly positive aspect of restructuring has been the growth of the private sector (see Table 2). Whereas total GDP fell by 12 per cent in 1990, the measured growth of the private sector was strongly positive: 7.4 per cent and as much as 17.5 per cent for the part of the private sector that existed prior to 1989. It is unclear how accurately private sector activity is measured. There are reasons to believe that it is understated. It is likely to be understated because many private activities are not recorded, either because they are not taxed or because the government's statistical reporting system is inadequate to the task. The activities in the "grey" economy are also inherently difficult to track. The underrecording of private sector activity — at least in the

Table 2. **Share of the private sector: main indicators, 1989-1991**

Percentage

	1989	1990	1991
GDP[1]	28.4	35.0	–
Employment			
Including private agriculture[2]	44.3	45.8	50.6
Excluding private agriculture[3]	29.5	30.9	36.7
External trade			
Total	–	8.6	36.2
Exports	–	4.9	21.9
Imports	–	14.4	49.9
Investment	35.3	41.3	–
Material production			
Industrial production	16.2	17.4	24.1
Construction[4]	33.4	32.2	55.2
Trade	59.5	63.7	82.8
Transport	11.5	14.2	23.7

1. In constant prices of 1984.
2. As share of total employment.
3. As share of non-agricultural employment.
4. Building and construction.
Source: Polish Central Statistical Office (GUS).

28

trade and transportation sectors, if not in industry — is inferred from general observation and the fact that unemployment is said to have increased by less than employment has decreased.

However impressive the growth of the private sector, it still remains small in absolute size and concentrated in services offered mainly by very small firms. The share of the private sector in total employment in medium to large-scale industrial enterprises was only about 1.2 per cent in 1990. The private sector's industrial activity in 1990 grew by only 0.4 per cent compared to 50.4 per cent for private domestic trading activities. The private sector is reported to have accounted for just over 20 per cent of total exports, mainly agricultural exports.

Moreover, while the growth of the private sector and the redirection of trade to the West represent notable structural changes, many characteristics of Poland's inherited industrial structure remain. They include:

— The *size distribution of firms* (see Charts 1.6 and 1.7 in the Annex). By comparison with advanced market economies, the size distribution of firms in post-socialist economies is skewed because too few small and medium size enterprises exist, and they account for too small a fraction of output and employment. This lopsidedness is likely to limit the opportunities for sub-contracting and for pursuing a niche competitive strategy.

— *Location patterns*. Poland's centrally planned regime tried to decentralise industry by establishing many heavy industries in rural regions. Now that these industries are in financial trouble, the regions in which they are located are in serious social and economic trouble as well.

— *High energy intensity and low energy efficiency* (see Table 1.17 in the Annex). Polish industry still consumes far more energy than its overseas equivalents and uses it relatively inefficiently. This has given rise to extremely low environmental standards, with respect to both air and water pollution (see Tables 1.18 to 1.21 and Chart 1.16 in the Annex).

— *Poor telecommunication infrastructure* (see Table 1.1 in the Annex). An efficient high-income economy requires good infrastructure, not least in telecommunication. Yet by OECD standards, Poland's telecommunication infrastructure is underdeveloped, although slowly improving.

II. Progress on systemic reforms

The agenda

Although observers may differ on the issues they emphasize, there is wide agreement on the agenda that must be followed if Poland is to develop a dynamic industrial sector. It is necessary:

— to orient Polish enterprise towards market structures, by ending the "soft budget constraint" and allowing demand and supply to determine product prices;

— to create a competitive environment, by introducing world market discipline and incentives and directing entrepreneurs and managers towards cost reduction and improved quality; and

— to fashion the institutional capabilities, both within and outside firms, that will allow Polish industry to compete. These capabilities are critical for product improvement and marketing and for science and technology. They must serve SMEs as well as large-scale enterprises.

Poland has made considerable progress in establishing a market economy, particularly in product markets. Product prices have largely been freed, and firms now operate virtually without subsidies. Except in the energy sector, the few subsidies that remain may be lower than those received on average by private firms in most OECD countries, where industrial subsidies typically represent 2-3 per cent of industrial value added.

This has taken political resolve, as one of the immediate effects of reform was a sharp rise in the prices of food, fuel, and transportation. These prices have risen because before 1989 the major subsidies were targeted to consumers for basic necessities (see Table 3). They were allocated directly far less to producers, and were largely for energy inputs.

Poland now faces the great task of moving ahead to establish a competitive environment and to create the institutional framework for becoming competitive by international standards. Only in this way can Poland create the entrepreneurial and employment opportunities necessary to offset the high costs of stabilisation and restructuring.

Poland's Economic Transformation Programme has relied on six measures to achieve both privatisation and restructuring of the industrial sector: 1) establishment of the basic legal infrastructure for developing a private industrial sector; 2) privatisation; 3) liberalisation of foreign investment; 4) trade liberalisation; 5) demonopolisation; and 6) financial reform. Each of these will be discussed briefly below.

Table 3. Government subsidies
(% of total State budget revenues)

	Total subsidies	Products & services	Producers	Municipalities & housing
1985	39.6	21.3	9.8	8.5
1986	39.5	24.2	5.9	9.4
1987	43.2	28.9	2.5	11.8
1988	41.6	29.4	3.7	8.5
1989	39.9	23.8	8.6	7.5
1990	16.8	8.2	5.9	2.7
1991*	10.7	5.4	1.9	3.4

* First eight months.

Structure of government subsidies
(%)

	1987	1988	1989	1990
Food products	21.4	30.6	28.3	2.8
Other consumer goods	4.4	2.5	1.9	1.4
Transportation	11.3	11.9	32.0	26.8
Foreign trade	15.7	13.8	1.9	---
Housing	22.6	15.6	18.9	38.0
Loss making enterprises	6.3	1.9	0.9	12.7
Other	18.3	23.7	16.1	18.3
Total	100	100	100	100

Source : Polish Ministry of Finance.

A. Property rights, company and bankruptcy laws

1. The new legal framework

The Polish constitution now guarantees the right to private property. Around 50 different laws govern the practical exercise of this basic right, in areas ranging from agricultural land transfer to urban land taxation. A draft reprivatisation law was prepared in 1991 to clarify the delicate question of the restitution of land or other economic assets to their former owners. It proposes, in particular, compensation in the form of capital vouchers convertible into shares of privatised enterprises.

The current company law in Poland is the Commercial code of 1934 which allows two corporate forms: the limited liability company and the joint stock company. State-owned enterprises only fall under the provisions of the code after incorporation (see the discussion of privatisation below). The joint stock firm follows German practice in establishing a two-tier board (a supervisory board is mandatory in companies with over 50 shareholders and 250 million zlotys in capital).

The current bankruptcy law stems from the Bankruptcy Act of 1934. It is applicable to any type of incorporated firm, but state-owned enterprises are also eligible for another procedure: liquidation under Article 19 of the Law on State-owned enterprises. The bankruptcy law resembles most legislation in continental Europe. It provides general procedures for both liquidation and reorganisation under the control of a court-appointed receiver. Bankruptcy is overseen by a tribunal of the local court. If a petition is accepted, the tribunal appoints a judge, who then appoints a trustee. The trustee manages the company with the mandatory co-operation of the original managers who lose their management rights.

2. The remaining shortcomings

Tremendous legislative work has been accomplished during the past two years, and all the basic elements of the legal framework and infrastructure of a market economy now exist in Poland. However, there is still room for improvement, especially in the areas of real property rights and bankruptcy procedures.

Inadequate definition and enforcement of real property rights in Poland threaten to act as a brake on the economic adjustment process, particularly for the development of the SME sector and foreign investment. Unless investors are assured of property ownership, use and transfer rights, they will prefer consumption or holding foreign assets. Present legislation is too complex and leaves certain issues unresolved. Thus, land or other property formerly under state ownership often now lacks clear title and is therefore unavailable for sale or long-term lease. Many uncertainties remain with regard to restitution principles and procedures. Implementation of the legislation presents serious bottlenecks. Poland's registry system is in disarray, the notarial system is slow and expensive, and the courts are not equipped to perform all their tasks rapidly.

The lack of bankruptcies is not only due to the weaknesses of the bankruptcy legislation and procedures. There are also important political and economic reasons, as the present report points out. Nonetheless, as the recent *OECD Economic Survey[1]* argued in detail, the current bankruptcy law may be too biased towards liquidation, as opposed to reorganisation, and therefore ill-adapted to Poland's restructuring needs. A better designed bankruptcy procedure, allied with strengthened institutional capabilities to implement it (e.g. the availability of receivers), is among the tools needed to promote industrial restructuring.

B. Privatisation

1. The multi-track approach

The Ministry of Ownership Changes (MOC) is largely responsible for privatisation. It has distinguished between privatisation through "transformation" (also called the "capital route"), and privatisation through "liquidation". In transformation, the state company remains an entity throughout the privatisation exercise, while in liquidation, the company is dissolved and its assets are leased or sold in one form or another to the owners of a new, distinct company (see Charts 6 and 7).

The enterprises chosen for privatisation through transformation are initially transformed into joint stock companies whose shares are owned by the Polish Treasury; this is the intermediate or "commercialisation" stage between public and private ownership. In commercialisation, a state-owned enterprise is converted into a corporate form with property rights vested in a corporate board of directors appointed by the owner, who is still the State Treasury, and eventually new private shareholders. When a state-owned enterprise has been commercialised, its workers' council is disbanded; instead, workers are given one-third of the seats (generally two) in the supervisory council. The shares of "commercialised" enterprises are then sold in one of three ways: 1) initial public offering, i.e. a traditional stock offering; 2) trade sale, in which a company is sold to a single investor through competitive bidding; or 3) mass privatisation.

Mass privatisation has several goals. First, to accelerate privatisation dramatically; this is seen as fundamental to improving the economy's ability to respond to market conditions. Second, to improve the efficiency and the value of several hundred Polish state-owned enterprises by converting them to joint stock companies; these would be transferred to new investment groups or financial intermediaries (which would eventually become mutual funds), that would be run with management skills and capital from Poland and abroad. Third, to give all adult citizens a stake in the privatisation process by issuing "vouchers" that can be exchanged for shares in the newly created investment groups; this would enable them to benefit from the (hopefully increasing) value of enterprises in a fair and equitable manner.

Chart 6. **THE PRIVATISATION PROCESS**

Overview

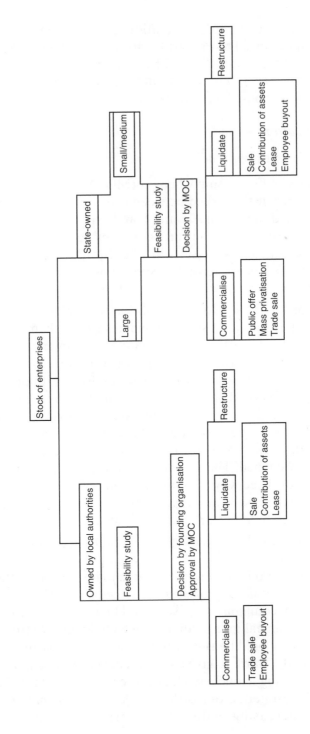

Note: MOC = Ministry of Ownership Changes.

Sources: Polish Ministry of Ownership Changes; World Bank.

Chart 7. TRANSFORMATION OF STATE-OWNED ENTERPRISES THROUGH PRIVATISATION / RESTRUCTURING / LIQUIDATION

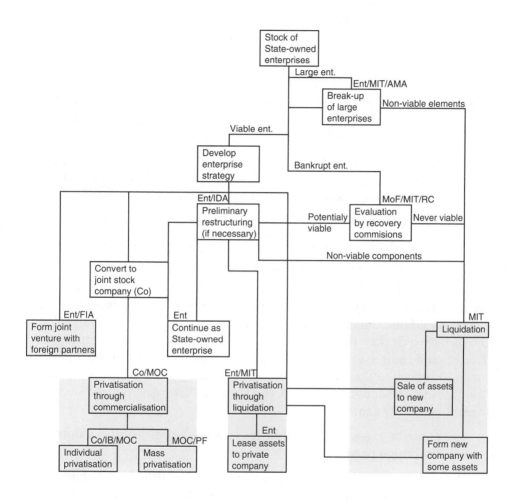

Key to responsible agencies:

Ent	Enterprises
MIT	Ministry of Industry and Trade
MOC	Ministry of Ownership Changes
AMA	Anti-Monopoly Agency
RC	Recovery Commission
MoF	Ministry of Finance
IDA	Industrial Development Agency
IB	Investment Bank
PF	Privatisation Fund
FIA	Foreign Investment Agency

Note: For more details see Charts 1.1 and 1.2 in the Annex.

Sources: Polish Ministry of Ownership Changes; World Bank.

The anticipated steps towards mass privatisation are as follows:

a) a number of investment funds will be formed, with Polish-led boards of directors;

b) discussions will begin with several international banks and fund managers who have expressed interest in managing the investment groups on the basis of management contracts;

c) certificates of participation in these investment funds will be distributed to all adult citizens at a later stage; but shares in the funds will only be traded after first yearly results;

d) as many as 400 medium to large-sized state-owned enterprises will be converted to joint stock companies, and a majority of their shares will be transferred to an investment fund;

e) these companies will be restructured and developed; and

f) financial support might be made available for the restructuring of these companies from the government and from abroad.

Privatisation through liquidation is intended for the smaller to medium firms. It may occur in two ways. If enterprises are insolvent, they can be liquidated under Article 19 of the law on state-owned enterprises at the initiative of the "founding organ" (often the Ministry of Industry and Trade), and their assets sold off to private enterprises or individuals, the proceeds going to the creditors. If, instead, they are solvent, they can be "liquidated" under Article 37 of the Law of Privatisation in one of two main ways. They can:

a) contribute assets and liabilities to a joint venture with a domestic or foreign partner; or

b) sell assets and liabilities to a new firm established by management and workers (buy-out), a method usually involving a transitional leasing arrangement with deferred interest payment facilities offered by the government.

It is to be noted that, whether the path is transformation or liquidation under Article 37, approval of the workers' council is required at the beginning of the process and that of the Ministry of Ownership Changes at the end. This ministry has taken a sectoral approach (sometimes improperly referred to as "sectoral privatisation") to managing the multi-track privatisation programme. With the help of foreign consulting firms, they collect and analyse industrial information on domestic and world markets. To date, 34 sectoral studies have been undertaken, primarily to be used to

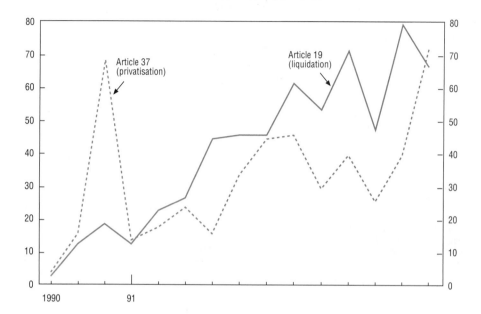

Chart 8. **APPLICATIONS FOR PRIVATISATION THROUGH LIQUIDATION**
Number of applications per month

Source : Polish Ministry of Ownership Changes.

accelerate and rationalise the process of individual sales. They will also serve as background information for the other types of privatisation.

2. *The privatisation record*

Poland's privatisation programme has very ambitious objectives. It aims to transfer half of the industrial state-owned assets to private owners within three years, and within five, to have an ownership structure identical to that of an average EC country. (The Law of Privatisation was passed in July 1990).

It is difficult to say precisely how much privatisation, particularly through liquidation, has occurred. It is clear, however, that it will be far behind schedule by mid-1992. In fact, only privatisation of small firms has proceeded as planned; by the end of September 1991, 75 per cent of trading firms, 45 per cent of construction firms and around 80 per cent of trucking were in private hands. In contrast, privatisation of medium to large industrial enterprises (numbering more than 8 000) has been much slower than expected.

37

Table 4.   **Summary of progress in privatisation**

	31.12.90	30.6.91	31.12.91	30.3.92
Total number of state-owned enterprises	8 453	8 591	8 228	8 273
Small/medium enterprises privatised by				
liquidation:	59	343	950	1 123
Under Article 37[1, 2]	37	170	416	488
Under Article 19[3]	22	173	534	635
Companies converted to joint-stock companies				
awaiting privatisation	159	162	244	504
Capital privatisation	1	13	26	32
including:				
Leveraged buy-outs	1	1	2	2
Public flotation	–	6	8	8
Trade sales	–	5	16	22

1. Of which approximately 90 per cent through leasing.
2. In 1991 including industry (85 firms), trade (79), construction (185).
3. In 1991 including industry (170 firms), trade (47), construction (86).
Source: Dynamika Prywatyzacji, Ministry of Ownership Changes, Warsaw, Nos. 6 and 8, 1992.

By the end of 1991, along the "capital route" intended for medium and large companies, fewer than 30 enterprises had been privatised through direct sales (16), public offerings (8), or leverage buy-outs (2); and the first phase of mass privatisation had not yet been launched. Mass privatisation was destined initially to affect 800 to 1 000 companies. This number was then reduced to 400 (including some 170 manufacturing firms or around 14 per cent of the employment in manufacturing — see Table 5). This first phase is now underway and planned to last through the autumn of 1992. It involves two tranches each of around 200 firms.

Privatisation of small and medium-sized firms has been comparatively successful (see Chart 8), especially through liquidation and sale to a new company established by management and workers, a method allowed under Article 37 of the Law of Privatisation. By the end of 1991, this method accounted for about 90 per cent of the 500 (including some 100 in industry) completed liquidations. In addition, around 600 firms (including some 100 in industry) had been liquidated under Article 19 of the Law on State-owned enterprises. In this case, in principle, assets are sold at auction, although the process does not seem always to have been transparent. There appear to have been a number of unofficial liquidations whereby former managers (some of them members of the *nomenklatura*) acquired the profitable parts of enterprises at very low price.

Table 5. **The first large privatisations**

1. Domestic public offerings

Name (Industry)	Public Offering	Share take-up in %			
		Domestic Institutions	Management Board	Employees	Foreign Investors
EXBUD S.A. (Construction)	45	---	17.5	20	17.5
SLASKA FABRYKA KABLI S.A. (Furniture)	70	---	---	20	10
PROCHNIK S.A. (Garment manufacturing)	57	17	---	20	6
KROSNO S.A. (Glass manufacturing)	50	28	---	20	2
TONSE S.A. (Audio equipment)	32	18	---	20	30

2. Leverage Buy-Outs

ZAKLADY MIESNE INOWROCLAW (meat processing)   Employees (100%)

3. Trade Sales

FAMPA S.A. (Textile machinery)   Single investor (80%) ; Employees (20%)

POLAN PILA S.A. (Lamps)   Single investor (51%) ; Employees (20%) ; State Treasury (29%)

Mass privatisation in industry
Sectoral breakdown of manufacturing enterprises concerned

Sectors	Number of enterprises	Employment	As % of total employment [2]
Metallurgy	7	14 100	8.0
Engineering	70	223 000	21.4
Minerals	10	10 600	5.5
Chemicals	25	45 900	18.4
Wood and paper	9	14 700	7.2
Light industry [1]	42	82 700	16.3
Food industry	4	6 800	1.6
Other	3	1 500	1.7
Total manufacturing	170	399 300	13.8

1.   Textiles, Clothing and Leather products.
2.   August 1991.

Sources : Polish Ministry of Industry and Trade (Promasz); World Bank.

The privatisation process involves many actors: management of enterprises, workers'councils, trade unions and often even a general assembly of employees; founding ministries; the Ministry of Ownership Changes (MOC); the Anti-Monopoly Office. However, at important stages it is centralised, major decisions being entrusted to the MOC. There is now a real risk that institutional bottlenecks will slow the privatisation process, even though other obstacles have probably played a greater role to date. A recent study2 observes that by the end of January 1991, the Ministry had received 139 applications for liquidation. Of these, 88 had entered the liquidation track a few months later. Of the 88, 31 enterprises in poor financial condition were accepted for liquidation, and their assets will be sold at auction, while 57 will have their assets leased to companies set up by former employees. The remaining 51 enterprises are still awaiting a decision by the Ministry. According to the study, such a centralised approach to privatisation poses the problem of the processing capacities of the Ministry, which may be unable to deal effectively with the growing number of applications.

It was partly in response to the limited capacity of the MOC to process a large number of applications for individual privatisation that the "mass privatisation" concept was devised. Despite the multi-track approach to privatisation, many state-owned enterprises — "orphans" in the queue for privatisation — still await action by the Ministry.

C. Foreign investment

1. A new liberal regime

Foreign investment is envisioned as a major pillar of privatisation. The Polish government anticipates that foreign investors will provide a large share of the capital, technology, and general managerial know-how necessary to support the transformation of state-owned enterprises into privately owned, efficient firms.

Recent legislation making the conditions for investment more attractive to foreigners removes earlier reservations about the share of a Polish enterprise that foreign investors should be allowed to own. In July 1991, a new law went into effect that enables foreign investors to transfer all their profits out of the country should they so wish. It also exempts them from the need to get a license and to make a minimum equity contribution in foreign currency (see Table 6).

Table 6. **Policy towards foreign investment in Central and Eastern European countries as of July 1991**

Country	Foreign ownership	Repatriation of profits	Field of activity	Investment incentives
Bulgaria	No set limit [1].	Profit transfer in hard currency is allowed.	All economic sectors, except where prohibited by law or similar authority.	No excise duty on imported capital goods or raw materials to be used for the purpose of the investment (min.level of foreign investment may be required). Some tax holidays depending on location and industry.
CCSFR	100% permitted with advance approval.	Part of foreign currency receipts must be offered to the State Bank; salaries and profits may be transferred abroad from hard currency resources of the JV.	All economic sectors, except those relating to defense or national security.	Selective incentives, depending on investment, including tax holidays and exclusion from antitrust suits.
Hungary	100% permitted.	Profit transfer in hard currency is allowed. Conversion of profits into hard currency guaranteed by the government.	All economic sectors.	Taxation incentives available for specific activities.
Poland	100% permitted.	100% of hard currency profit remittable; government can authorize remittance of zloty profits.	All economic sectors.	Capital expenditures may be charged against taxable profits. No excise duty on imported capital goods which form part of a shareholder's capital contribution or are purchased within 3 years of the company's establishment. Tax holidays.
Romania	100% permitted with advance approval.	Partial profit transfer in hard currency allowed.	Foreign investment forbidden if it affects national security and defense or if it would infringe on environmental law.	Tax holidays depending on sector. Foreign contributions in kind are duty free.

1. Minimum capital requirement of $20 000 or $550 000 for banks.
Source : US Office of Technology Assessment.

41

Chart 9. **FOREIGN INVESTMENT IN CENTRAL AND EASTERN EUROPE**

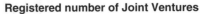

Registered number of Joint Ventures

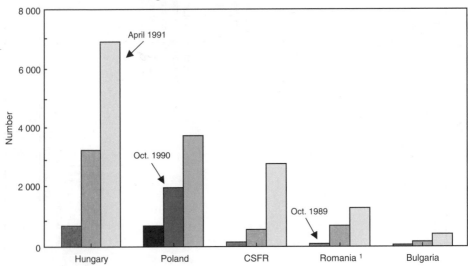

1. There were five Joint Ventures registered in Romania as of Oct. 1989.

Source: UN Economic Commission for Europe.

Foreign capital outlay in registered Joint Ventures

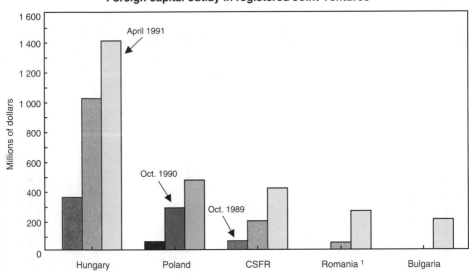

1. Estimated capital outlays were not available for Romania in 1989 nor for Bulgaria in 1989 and 90.

Source: UN Economic Commission for Europe.

To make foreign investment still easier, accounting standards has been brought into line with those of the EC. (Poland's tax system is also being reformed to conform more to that prevailing in the EC, i.e. a general income tax has been introduced and a value added tax will be implemented in 1993.)

2. The foreign investment record

One reason why privatisation has been slower than anticipated is that less direct foreign investment has flowed into Poland than was initially expected. In the competition among PIT countries to attract foreign investment, Poland has some advantages (e.g. the largest market, the richest natural resources endowment) but also some handicaps, a certain number of which are related to the policy context: unstable bureaucracy, unclear ownership status for real estate, uncertainties surrounding tax policies, the mistrustful attitude of extreme political forces.

The most dynamic developments in the area of foreign investment concern joint ventures. According to data from the Agency for Foreign Investment, 4 850 licenses for the formation of companies with foreign participation had been issued by the end of June 1991. Of these, 2 130 were joint ventures. The largest numbers of shareholders in joint venture companies were from the Federal Republic of Germany (1 330), the USA (357), Sweden (339), Austria (295), and the Netherlands (274). Joint ventures operate primarily in services, trade with foreigners, trade in fruits and vegetables, wholesale trade in consumer goods, and the manufacture of apparel and plastic goods. It is worth noting that relatively few joint ventures are in the industrial sector.

The average value of foreign investments in Poland, whether joint venture or otherwise, is quite small. The total amount of foreign investment at the end of June 1991 was only $580 million ($280 million of this was in four contracts), or about $133 000 per established company, since the majority of joint ventures started with the minimum capital requirement ($50 000) (see Chart 9). According to the latest statistics, joint ventures and direct acquisitions of Polish firms amounted to $670 million in total by October 1991. (Since then several large contracts in the automotive sector have been signed.)

Inflows of foreign debt capital have also been slow. This is discussed below in an assessment of Poland's new financial institutions.

. *Trade liberalisation*

1. *Border opening and abolition of the State monopoly on foreign trade*

Trade liberalisation in Poland has included establishing internal convertibility of the zloty, reducing and rationalising customs tariffs and abolishing the State's monopoly on foreign trade. These radical changes have been supported by a $1 billion stabilisation fund to support the zloty and by the Paris Club Agreement to reduce the present value of debt by 50 per cent. Particularly important has been agreement to reduce interest payments to 1994. Together with strong trade performance, these measures have helped to reestablish reserves.

Low customs tariffs were put into effect in 1990. They were lifted altogether on about 80 per cent of the 5000 items on the customs list. The average nominal tariff was reduced to about 10 per cent, and the actual average tariff barrier is estimated to have amounted to no more than 5 per cent.

Low tariffs, long suppressed demand for foreign goods, and the removal of quantitative restrictions led to a sharp rise in imports towards the end of 1990. Imports of consumer goods were especially strong in the first eight months of 1991: as a share of total imports, consumer goods rose from 18.8 per cent in 1990 to 31.6 per cent.

In August 1991, tariffs were raised, partly because of the negative consequences, especially on small and medium enterprises, of excessive import liberalisation. The new tariff schedule is based on the so-called combined nomenclature of the EC, which specifies that the tariff level on a particular product depends on the country and region of origin, as stipulated in GATT regulations. The average tariff in Poland is now 14.2 per cent.

2. *The foreign trade record*

In 1988, only some 100 foreign trade organisations (FTOs) plus some 800 foreign trade offices in large manufacturing firms traded with the rest of the world. Today, tens of thousands do so, and more than 80 per cent are believed to be private organisations.

In 1991, the export of industrial products showed more dynamism than the production of industrial products. By comparison with 1978, the value of exports was about 40 per cent higher in 1991 while the value of production was about 25 per cent lower. Beginning in 1989, there was a significant acceleration in exports to non-CMEA countries. With a simultaneous fall in the absolute value of trade with the CMEA, the proportions of trade with the CMEA and non-CMEA areas changed dramatically. Following trade liberalisation, Polish industry has thus entered the world market very rapidly. Increased imports have been decisive for ending consumer shortages, for alleviating supply shortages in production, and for strengthening market discipline among domestic producers.

Despite the significant gains due to trade liberalisation, there have also been some negative signs. The balance of payments surplus achieved in 1990 has become an important deficit in the first half of 1991. Comparing the first eight months of 1991 to 1990, foreign trade calculated in current prices showed a large increase in imports while exports decreased. The prices obtained from exports rose by 13.7 per cent while the prices paid for imports increased by 30.9 per cent, which meant a deterioration of 13 points in the terms of trade.

This deterioration was largely due to a shift to world prices and to hard currency for oil and gas trade with the ex-USSR republics. In 1989, the USSR took over 30 per cent of the Polish exports and it now takes virtually none. In the first two months of 1991, Poland paid $250 million for imports from the ex-USSR and received only $20 million for its exports.

Moreover, changes in the composition of trade do not bode very well for long-run economic development. The share of exports in engineering and light consumer products declined, while that of metallurgy products increased by about 90 per cent. Yet metallurgy tends to be a highly polluting industry — although technical rehabilitation, as planned by the government, can improve the situation — and it uses non-renewable resources. In the composition of imports, consumer goods rose sharply.

E. Demonopolisation

1. The new legal and institutional framework

Poland's heritage of centrally planned production and distribution created the risk that when economic units become independant undertakings, they would enter the newly created market with dominant or monopolistic positions. The danger of monopoly came from two sources. First, where a former state undertaking was the only producer of certain goods, the danger of monopoly was obvious. Second, there was the danger that the State agencies formerly responsible for overseeing enterprises would appear in market conditions as organisers of cartels. To promote competition, an Anti-Monopoly Office was established in April 1990. In early

. employed 106 people, mainly lawyers and economists. The Anti-monopoly Office participates in the government's privatisation efforts by seeking to prevent private monopolies from replacing former state monopolies and by promoting competition by improving conditions for the formation of new enterprises.

To support the development of competition, the Anti-Monopoly Office disposes of a structural and a regulatory function. The structural function depends on its power to affect:

— the division of large firms;

— the formation of joint stock companies (the first stage in the privatisation of state-owned enterprises);

— the creation of new businesses;

— the prevention of the formation of cartels; and

— the prevention of the formation of monopolies.

The regulatory function rests on its power to challenge abusive monopolistic practices such as price gouging, agreements among firms to limit competition, and imposition of difficult contractual conditions, e.g. "tie-in" contracts, whereby a firm makes a contract conditional on the fulfillment of an unrelated condition.

2. The anti-monopoly record

The Anti-Monopoly Office has acted vigorously to control practices that violate the rules of competition. Between April and December 1990 it considered 200 cases related to monopolistic practices (tie-in contracts, price gouging) and 261 cases of merger and restructuring activity endangering competition. It considered 13 appeals. Finally, it established a list of enterprises holding monopolistic positions in order to facilitate price monitoring.

Given the need to build legislation and institutions from scratch, these are impressive achievements. Of course, as Anti-Monopoly Office's studies have found, not all parts of the Polish economy are highly concentrated. In particular, the Office's Economic Data Analysis Unit found that there was not high concentration in the production of textiles, clothing, foods, ceramics, and cosmetics. This last finding is confirmed by a study by the consulting firm Bain and Company which showed that in 1991, the Polish detergent production was much more fragmented than in western Europe, and the detergent companies were operating at sub-efficient scale. (see Chart 1.8 in the Annex).

Effective competition should not be measured by the static distribution of domestic market shares but by the "contestability" of the relevant market, i.e. the extent to which alternative suppliers, including foreign ones, can squeeze monopoly profits through competition. The Anti-Monopoly Office has been active within the government in arguing against tariffs and other trade barriers. Increasing integration into world markets thanks to trade liberalisation means that world competitive structures must be considered when deciding on changes in domestic industrial organisation. Breaking up of large firms does not always coincide with the needs of competition policy: sustained competition in the market may require that firms be sufficiently large to exploit economies of scale and scope. Equally there are many cases where firms should be broken up on efficiency rather than competition grounds.

In the definition and treatment of cartelisation, the Polish anti-monopoly law only partly distinguishes between horizontal agreements (i.e. agreements between competitors) and vertical agreements, which do not involve competitors. As the Anti-Monopoly Office recognises, prohibiting vertical agreements, even in the particular conditions of Poland, is more likely to slow the development of competition than to increase its extent and effectiveness[3].

F. Financial reform

1. The creation of a two-tiered banking system and of a financial market

Poland's financial system was considered a major cause of the "economy of shortage" in the years prior to 1989. The financial system was therefore a focus for reform efforts after 1989. Within a framework influenced by the International Monetary Fund, the "Balcerowicz Stabilisation Plan" that took effect in January 1990 was designed to reduce the public sector budget deficit and introduce positive real interest rates.

To implement this plan, the government established a two-tier banking system, composed of the National Bank of Poland, which plays the role of central bank and supervises the banking system, and commercial banks, which serve both individuals and public and private enterprises. In addition, a financial market for government bonds was established, and a capital market, consisting initially of a Stock Exchange was opened in April 1991 and quoted nine companies as of November 1991.

Nine commercial banks were created out of the regional branches of the former National Bank of Poland, but remain state banks. However, there are plans to privatise two of the commercial banks in 1992.

Private banks are still small and local. Some new ones are being created as joint ventures between private and state capital, such as the Kredyt Bank SA of Warsaw. Only five foreign banks operated in Poland at the end of 1991. Citibank is the only major foreign bank doing business in Poland.

2. The financial reform record

Creating an efficient capital market is an immense task, particularly under a strictly enforced anti-inflationary stabilisation plan. By the end of 1991, a large and growing number of Polish enterprises were financially insolvent. This meant a large number of non-performing loans for the banking system. By end March 1992, nearly 1 300 major industrial enterprises had lost their creditworthiness. Not surprisingly, the growth of financial intermediation has been relatively slow.

For one, high real interest rates have discouraged the demand for loans while a high level of interest capitalisation has reduced the supply of new funds available for lending. Newly created private firms continued to grow in 1991, by 33 per cent as compared with 1990. Nevertheless, a survey conducted in the Gdansk region showed that only 19 per cent used bank credit as a source of initial capital[4]. The rest came from personal savings (73 per cent) and family and friends (27 per cent). As noted earlier, most of these private enterprises are not in the industrial sector; those in the industrial sector have had a very high bankruptcy rate.

A high rate of self-financing and bankruptcy is to be expected among newly formed firms in a highly depressed economic milieu. But the fact that small firms cannot rely for some start-up capital on the banking system means that entrepreneurship tends to be restricted to the group in society that managed to accumulate some wealth under the old economic system or from trading in the last two years.

Moreover, a lack of intermediation on the part of the banking system has slowed the processing of foreign loans, and a substantial part are underutilised. The Ministry of Finance attributes this underutilisation partly to the inexperience of the newly established Polish banks.

Table 7. **Restructuring and privatisation of industry**
Programmes and actions

	PRIVATISATION	RESTRUCTURING	
		Rationalisation of industrial structure	Management of State-owned enterprises
Objectives	. Medium term: attain within five years an ownership structure identical to that of an average EC country. . Shorter term: transfer within three years to private owners half of the industrial state-owned enterprises using multitrack approach (individual transactions, liquidation, mass privatisation). . Comprehensive strategy adopted in Feb. 1991.	. Liquidate non-viable SOEs. . Break-up monopolies and overly integrated enterprises. . Promote restructuring of viable SOEs in the cases where private investors cannot be found and where mass privatisation is not applicable in the short term. . Promote development of industrial SMEs.	. Corporatise (conversion into joint-stock companies) SOEs to introduce adequate corporate governance. . Introduce mechanisms for effective management of State assets. . Impose effective hard budget constraint on the SOEs management.
Key legislation	. 1934 Commercial Code. . Law on Economic Activity (Jan. 1989). . Privatisation Law for State-owned enterprises (SOEs) (July 1990, Nov. 1990). . Anti-Monopoly Act (Feb. 1990) . Law on Foreign Investment (July 1991) [Replaces the Law on Joint Ventures (Dec. 1988, Dec. 1989)].	. Law on Bankrupcy (1934 Bankruping Act, Nov. 1981, Dec. 1989) . Anti-Monopoly Act (Feb. 1990). . Employment Law (Dec. 1989).	- Prior to 1989. . Laws establishing SOEs as self-governing and self-financing units (Sept. 1981, Feb. 1982 and 1987). - Since 1989 . Law on the financial management of SOEs (Jan. 1989). . Law on co-operatives (1990).
Key institutions	. Ministry of Ownership Changes (MOC). . Ministry of Industry and Trade (MIC). . Anti-Monopoly Agency (AMA). . Foreign Investment Agency (FIA). . Polish Development Bank (PDB).	. Ministry of Industry and Trade (MIT). . Anti-Monopoly Agency (AMA). . Industrial Development Agency (IDA). . Polish Development Bank (PDB).	. Ministry of Industry and Trade (MIT). . Ministry of Ownership Changes (MOC). . Ministry of Finance (MF).

Table 7. **Restructuring and privatisation of industry** (cont'd)

Actions	. 7 enterprises privatised through public offering of shares. . Few dozens of enterprises sold to foreign investors and/or employees. . 800 authorisations of privatisation through liquidation issued by MOC. . Small privatisation: over 80% of retailing in private hands.	. MIT has set up an enterprise monitoring system to give early warning of enterprises facing financial difficulties. . By mid-1991 MIT had liquidated 23 enterprises and bankrupted 3 enterprises. . MIT has completed sectoral restructuring studies. . IDA has completed individual firm restructuring studies. . MIT has created (in May 1990) the council for Entrepreneurship promotion.	. Selection and training by MOC of board members to represent State in the supervisory board of the enterprises which become commercialised on the way to becoming privatised. . Preparation of guidelines for the supervisory boards members. . Selection, training and appointment of a number of new SOEs managers.
In preparation or under discussion	. Mass privatisation (400 SOEs concerned): first stage includes 204 enterprises (of which 170 industrial) to be privatised through the "voucher" and "equity funds" system. . "Sectoral" privatisation: preparatory studies completed or nearing completion. . Commercialisation and management contracts to increase the value of SOEs to private investors. . Foreign Investment promotion programme being prepared by FIA.	. Establishment of an interministerial task-force to help speeding discussion on critical restructuring cases. . Improvement of the liquidation capabilities of MIT. . Development of a network of regional development agencies. . IDA to expand its program and in 1991/92 undertake 150 diagnosis studies and 100 full restructuring studies. . Preparation of programmes for sector-wide. groups of enterprises and regional restructuring.	. Preparation of a "Law on State Treasury" which would rule the management of assets which will remain in state hands. . Elaboration of new incentives to force SOEs to "commercialise".
Major obstacles	. Lack of domestic investment resources. . Lack of foreign investors' interest. . Worker councils and management's attitude. . High level of indebtedness of most SOEs. . Lack of human and financial resources available to government to manage a complex process. . Legal uncertainties regarding the ownership of SOEs assets. . Problems of coordination between the key institutions involved.	. High social and economic barriers to entry and exit. . Financial situation of SOEs often does not reflect long term economic viability. . Lack of resources to manage and finance restructuring at the firm or gouvernment level. . Weakness of the Polish banking sector. . Regional concentration of most acute restructuring problems.	. Shortage of trained personel to manage the SOEs in the new market environment. . Worker councils and management's attitude. . Complexity of the political and institutional context.

Sources : OECD; World Bank.

Chapter 2

Structural adjustment needs and outlook

Poland faces immense industrial adjustment needs:

— resources must be reallocated among enterprises, sectors and locations along sound economic principles;

— important technology and productivity gaps in most enterprises and sectors must be covered; and

— pro-market infrastructures must be developed to support adjustment and increase the international competitiveness of firms.

Polish industrial structure is characterised by allocative inefficiencies resulting from the past distorted structure of prices (especially the massive subsidising of energy), lack of competition and of incentives to workers and management. Politicised investment decisions at national and CMEA levels aggravated further the consequences of centrally planned resource allocation. Decentralisation of investment initiatives in the 1980s did not significantly alter the basic sectoral distribution of the capital stock. The emergence of a self-managed enterprise sector, in a market environment that remained highly regulated, has precipitated across-the-board decapitalisation (capital stock obsolescence), rather than reallocation of resources.

I.   The dimensions of the adjustment problem

Poland's "adjustment gap" is characterised by overdevelopment of heavy, energy-intensive industry at the expense of lighter industry and services; it will have to be filled if Poland is to take full advantage of its latent comparative advantages. At the same time, while the fundamental problems are clear, it is both difficult and inappropriate to attempt to predict the industrial profile that market forces will define. However, the major determining factors can be pointed out and their interplay described in a simplified medium term scenario for structural change in industry. The scenario can serve as a background for assessing, for policy purposes, the current structural adjustment issues.

The task of reshaping Polish industry is enormous. Industries which were sheltered in closed markets are now exposed to international competition. This reveals their weak "non-price competitiveness" which is due to outdated production and product technologies, deficient distribution channels, and the absence of marketing capabilities and established brand names. Changes in relative prices (to world terms) undermine the "price-competitiveness" and profitability of many enterprises.

Moreover, the collapse of highly specialised CMEA trade relationships has left Poland with production capacities in segments of many industrial sectors which have almost no value in the new market environment. And environmental considerations dictate the immediate closing down of some plants. The implementation of stringent regulations for emission of pollutants will increase the cost of restructuring and will often make closing down the only alternative [5].

If a single figure could give a broad idea of the magnitude of long-term industrial adjustment needs, it would be the number of industrial jobs that have to be redeployed if Poland's economic structure is to conform to that of an average mature developed market economy. At the beginning of the transition process, as Chart 10 shows, industrial employment per capita was far higher in Poland than in the European Community. Compared with their EC equivalents, nearly all Polish industries employed relatively more people, especially in the food, textile, clothing, leather products and footwear industries. The only exceptions were the paper and printing industries and parts of chemical and allied industries.

Assuming that industrial employment in Poland adjusts to the EC "standard", a reduction of roughly one million jobs in manufacturing — or almost one-third of the existing manufacturing jobs in 1989 — would be required (almost 500 000 were already lost between 1989 and mid-1991). How many jobs will really be lost depends on the evolution of the capital/labour ratio under the influence of price factors and technological catching-up, on growth trends in domestic demand, and on the competitive position that different Polish industries are able to retain or acquire in the international division of labour.

It is unclear whether the restructuring process should create less labour-intensive industrial specialisation, given that cheap labour is now Poland's main source of comparative advantage. But it must certainly

Chart 10.

Structure of GDP and employment by activity
1987

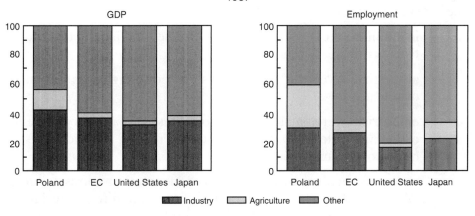

Sources: OECD; UNIDO; Eurostat; IFO.

Industrial employment per capita
in Poland, CSFR, and the European Community
1989

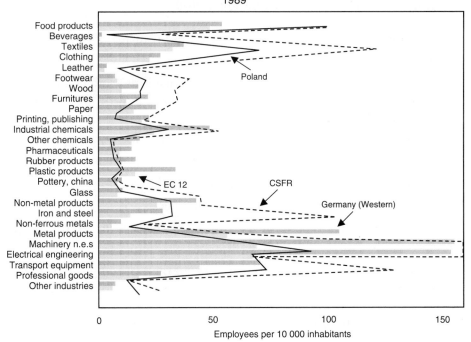

Sources: Polish Ministry of Industry and Trade (Promasz); Federal Ministry of Economy (CSFR); Eurostat.

53

entail an across-the-board increase in productivity, through the disappearance of the overstaffing resulting from the industrial and labour-market organisation and management systems of the past. Present overstaffing is due to several factors:

— in a non-market environment, enterprises had insufficient incentives to minimise costs;

— at the firm level, the planning system led to high administrative overheads;

— enterprises were entrusted with social tasks (health services, education and child care, transportation, recreation and sports, distribution of consumer goods, etc.);

— chronic shortages of materials and investment goods reduced labour productivity in general (workers waited for materials or equipment) and encouraged inefficient vertical integration and over-enlargement of departments in charge of repairs and tool-making.

II. Demand scenario for the transition period

Economic liberalisation and the associated transformations are bringing about major changes in the structure of final demand:

— the structure of current consumption, resulting from changed relative prices and the increased availability of new products, due largely to trade liberalisation;

— the structure of demand for capital goods, due in particular to the variable impact of adjustment on individual investor groups; and

— the overall structure of demand, especially the relationship between consumption and investment.

Individual demand categories will be variously affected during the three main phases in the adjustment process (see Table 8):

— The opening phase, now over, was characterised by the introduction of democratic institutions and rules in the political field, and by trade, market and price liberalisation supported by restrictive monetary and fiscal policy in the economic field.

— The current and critical adjustment phase consists of the actual restructuring process: privatisation, creation of institutions neces-

Table 8. **Demand patterns during the transition towards a market economy**

Industry	Main product category	Share of domestic market	Demand trend in		
			Phase I	Phase II	Phase III
Food products	CON	15.2		-	+
Beverages	CON	2.9		-	+
Tobacco	CON	2.1		-	+
Textiles	INT	4.8		-	+
Clothing	CON	2.4		-	+
Leather	INT	0.3		-	+
Footwear, leather goods	CON	0.8		-	+
Wood, wood products	INT	1.9		-	++
Furnitures	CON	1.5	-	--	++
Paper & pulp	INT	1.8		++	+
Paper products	INT	1.8		+	+
Printing, publishing	INT	3.9	+	+++	++
Basic chemicals	MAT	8.1	-	--	+
Pharmaceuticals	CON	1.8		+	+
Chemicals for households	CON	1.7		+	+
Rubber products	INT	1.2		-	+
Plastic products	INT	2.3		+	+
Pottery, china	INT	0.6		-	+
Glass products	INT	0.9		-	++
Non-metal products	MAT	2.9	-	--	++
Iron and steel	MAT	4.1	-	---	+
Non-ferrous metals	MAT	2.4	-	---	+
Foundries	INT	0.9	-	---	+
Metal products	INT	1.6	-	---	+
Steel construction	CAG	1.1	---	---	++
Boilermaking	CAG	1.0	---	---	+++
Metal articles	INT	2.7	-	---	+
Agricultural machinery	CAG	0.7	--	---	++
Machine tools	CAG	0.7	---	---	+++
Textile, clothing mach.	CAG	0.2	---	-	++
M. f. food and chemical industries	CAG	0.6	---	-	+++
M. f. mining and construction	CAG	1.2	---	-	+++
M. f. other industries	CAG	0.4	---	--	++
Machinery n.e.s	INT	3.0	--	---	++
Electrical equipment	CAG	2.3	---	--	+++
Lamps, lighting	CON	0.2	-		+
Elec. household appliances	CON	0.8		-	++
Consumer electronics	CON	1.7	++	+	+++
Telecommunication equipment	CAG	2.7	++	++	+++
Electronic Data Processing equip.	CAG	2.8	++	++	+++
Motor vehicles	CON	6.1	+	++	++
Shipbuilding	CAG	0.7	-	---	+
Locomotives, wagons	CAG	0.2	-	---	+++
Air & space equipment	CAG	1.4	-	---	++
Professional goods	CAG	0.8	-	--	++
Toys, sports goods	CON	0.9	-	--	++
Total manufacturing		100.0	-	--	++

CAG = Capital goods;   CON = Consumer goods;   INT = Intermediates;   MAT = Material;
+ = rising   - = declining
++ = pronounced rise   -- = pronouced decline
+++ = boom   --- = collapse
Sources : OECD, IFO.

55

sary for the functioning of a market economy, restructuring of foreign trade relations and adjustment of industrial structures to the new patterns of demand and competition. This phase is accompanied by great socio-economic friction, due in part to a steep rise in unemployment.

— The third phase will be the recovery. New supply structures will take shape. The modernisation of infrastructure, especially for energy and telecommunications, will accelerate and begin to have a sizeable positive impact on economic performance. This phase will see a dynamic growth process with increases in production, domestic and foreign investment, employment, productivity, real wages and incomes.

In the first phase (*border and market opening, price liberalisation, macroeconomic stabilisation*), demand for previously hard-to-obtain consumer durables (cars, consumer electronics) and unavailable (COCOM list) capital goods (computer devices, mobile telephones) from the West was buoyant. But demand for most investment goods collapsed. A main reason was the paralysis of decision-making, resulting from the adjustment shock, in state-owned enterprises. A substantial portion of demand was initially directed towards second-hand goods imported from western European countries.

During the second phase (*restructuring*), demand for consumer goods suffers from the economic recession and the fear of unemployment, which leads households to refrain from purchases of major consumer durables. The market for capital goods remains flat. The demand for machinery and equipment is particularly weak, but foreign direct investment is able to stimulate demand in isolated cases. The urgently needed modernisation of the infrastructure proceeds only gradually because of political turbulence and financial difficulties. Housing construction is frozen, in particular because of uncertainties surrounding property rights, the low level of rents, and the fragility and immaturity of financing channels. The only dynamic portion of demand emanates from the still small but rapidly growing private small business sector.

In the third phase (*recovery*), demand will rebound and diversify to the benefit of the service sector. The catching-up process for the acquisition of consumer durables will take off on a large scale. There will be a boom in demand for capital goods (machinery and equipment, infrastructural facilities). In the course of wealth accumulation, household demand for housing and services will establish itself on a steady growth path.

III. Inherited industrial specialisation patterns

International trade and production statistics make it possible to identify the comparative advantages of different countries and areas of specialisation. But they do not give precise information about the mix of factors that explain competitive advantages, especially the qualitative factors of competitiveness such as technological novelty, product quality and reliability, the availability of an efficient distribution and service system, delivery time, and general company image.

The assessment of the competitiveness of the industrial activities of the former CMEA countries is even more difficult than for market economies. Analysis can only mark off the areas where industrial tradition, skilled labour and a technological basis create a potential competitive advantage that might be consolidated and exploited in the future.

A. *Inherited industrial employment structure and export specialisation*

The current sectoral employment profile of Polish industry is presented in Table 9. It is compared with that of the CSFR and the European Community, using a standard index of specialisation.

In the manufacturing sector, Poland is specialised in food processing, textiles, clothing and footwear, wood and wood processing, glass, iron and steel, non-ferrous metallurgy, transport equipment (motor vehicles and shipbuilding), and professional goods. To a certain extent the pattern resembles that of less developed market economies with rich natural resources, but it is idiosyncratic in many respects. It reflects in particular:

— specific features of final demand, which has a high share of low value added products, especially food products, in private consumption, and an artificially low level and sophistication of demand in business and households for written communication and packaging (with a consequent underdevelopment of the paper, printing and publishing sector); and

— the dual structure of industrial trade which prevailed until 1989 (the high share of intra-CMEA trade and the limited role of pure market mechanisms in trade with OECD countries).

The latter factor makes overall trade patterns a poor indicator of Polish comparative advantage. However, the structure of Polish exports to OECD countries is worth considering because it shows which industries

Table 9. **Industrial employment structure**

| | Employment 1990 | | | | Index of Specialisation [1] | |
| | In thousands | | Share in % | | | |
Industry	Poland	CSFR	Poland	CSFR	Poland	CSFR
Food products	417	168	12.3	7.0	138	79
Beverages	10	34	0.9	1.4	202	333
Textiles	290	200	8.9	8.3	152	142
Clothing	195	93	6.0	3.9	144	93
Leather	41	25	1.3	1.0	248	205
Footwear	88	67	2.7	2.8	188	194
Wood products	84	56	2.6	2.3	148	133
Furnitures	80	59	2.5	2.5	115	115
Paper	43	45	1.3	1.9	46	66
Printing, publishing	35	28	1.1	1.2	31	33
Industrial chemicals	133	89	4.1	3.7	92	83
Other chemicals	33	13	1.0	0.5	68	36
Pharmaceuticals	26	14	0.8	0.6	44	32
Rubber products	32	27	1.0	1.1	55	63
Plastic products	47	8	1.4	0.3	48	11
Pottery, china	23	10	0.7	0.4	60	36
Glass	47	73	1.4	3.0	121	254
Non-metal products	135	75	4.2	3.1	86	64
Iron and steel	136	168	4.2	7.0	143	240
Non-ferrous metals	58	24	1.8	1.0	156	88
Metal products	224	164	6.9	6.8	68	67
Mechanical engineering	385	500	11.8	20.8	95	168
Electrical engineering	233	189	7.2	7.9	62	68
Transport equipment	301	204	9.3	8.5	119	109
Professional goods	72	20	2.2	0.8	128	48
Other industries	83	46	2.6	1.9	252	189
Total manufacturing	3 349	2 779	100.0	100.0	100	100

1. Ratio of the industry's employment share in the country considered to the corresponding share in the EC (EC share = 100).

Sources : OECD; Eurostat; Polish and CSFR official sources.

Table 10. **Export specialisation** [1]

	Share of exports (1988, in %)			First index of specialisation [2]			Second index of specialisation [3]	
	OECD	CMEA [4]	USSR	CMEA [4]	CSFR	Poland	CSFR	Poland
Mining	7.7	6.0	477	268	62	264	79	336
Radio-actives	0.2	0.0	653	313	8	0	244	14
Oil refining	3.7	1.8	843	585	172	43	49	12
Food products	6.6	9.7	24	87	98	265	67	182
Tobacco	0.4	0.1	0	9	0	10	0	55
Textiles	4.3	5.9	17	78	171	79	126	59
Clothing	2.7	7.9	4	154	201	311	69	106
Leather	0.3	0.1	4	24	6	6	13	15
Footwear	1.1	2.1	1	95	248	207	136	114
Wood products	1.1	2.7	396	321	619	338	244	133
Furnitures	0.9	4.5	13	269	253	324	50	64
Paper & pulp	2.2	1.4	56	59	196	43	316	70
Paper products	0.5	0.3	1	34	57	7	88	10
Printing, publishing	0.6	0.4	6	35	129	7	210	12
Chemicals	10.4	10.8	54	80	115	74	110	71
Rubber products	1.0	1.0	3	53	156	54	156	54
Plastic products	1.8	0.9	3	29	83	30	158	57
Pottery, china	0.4	0.8	3	108	220	99	107	48
Glass	0.6	2.0	40	192	840	212	252	64
Non-metal products	1.3	1.2	35	64	152	67	167	74
Iron and steel	3.2	6.9	85	152	291	107	136	50
Non-ferrous metals	2.4	4.6	278	233	35	264	18	136
Foundries	0.1	0.2	42	101	113	179	72	114
Metal products	0.9	1.2	15	73	140	158	110	124
Metal articles	2.0	2.1	7	58	77	79	74	75
Steel construction	0.5	0.6	32	76	49	164	41	139
Mechanical engineering	9.4	4.7	9	30	77	36	153	72
Electrical engineering	10.8	4.4	6	24	30	29	74	72
Motor vehicles	12.1	2.1	19	18	27	26	160	152
Shipbuilding	0.8	0.6	6	44	3	378	4	478
Air & space equipment	2.1	0.2	2	5	0	7	2	77
Professional goods	2.1	0.6	7	17	21	16	80	62
EDP equipment	3.9	0.2	1	3	2	1	38	26
Jewellery, toys, sports goods	1.8	1.2	143	102	109	32	167	48
Total manufacturing	100.0	100.0	100	100	100	100	100	100

1. Measured for exports to OECD countries.
2. The index is calculated on the basis of the structure of world exports to OECD.
3. The index is calculated on the basis of the structure of CMEA exports to OECD.
4. Excluding USSR.

Sources : OECD; IFO.

it gives a prominent place to material- or labour-intensive activities, especially clothing, wood and wood products, non-ferrous metallurgy and food processing. Fabricated metals (steel construction, foundry products) account for a larger share of exports to the OECD area than of production. Except for shipbuilding, Poland does not show any area of export specialisation in the more advanced manufacturing activities. The large engineering sector (almost one-fifth of total manufacturing employment) has been oriented far more than the average towards the domestic and CMEA markets.

The second specialisation index presented in Table 10 depicts intra-CMEA specialisation in servicing western markets. It confirms Poland's relatively weak position in engineering, especially when compared to that of the CSFR, and its marked specialisation in the production of transport equipment. Part of the explanation lies in deeply rooted industrial traditions and in the R&D policies pursued by central planners.

B. Specialisation in the light of R&D activities

Measuring R&D output and comparing the productivity and economic impact of national innovation systems is one of the most delicate tasks of applied economics. But, at a time when the role played by non-price determinants in the economic performance of firms, regions, and nations is increasing, it is also one of the most important. Innovation based on R&D is crucial to international competitiveness in the so-called science-based industries, i.e. parts of the chemical and metallic and non-metallic minerals sectors and a large portion of the durable goods industry.

Data derived from patent documents are the most widely used source for monitoring and comparing national R&D activity, because they allow comparable and detailed measurement of R&D output. The statistics of the IFO (Institut für Wirtschaftsforschung, Munich) are used here[6]. They only record innovations for which a patent application has been filed in at least two countries. The restriction eliminates most of the distortions in patent data[7], including those due to international differences in patent systems[8]. In the present context, it ensures that inventions from Central and Eastern Europe are taken into consideration only if they can be expected to meet the standards of quality of Western countries.

Table 11 shows Poland's position in industrial innovation competition during the 1980s, as measured by various indicators. Compared to the other two Partners in Transition (PIT) countries and to the former GDR, Poland has traditionally had weak patent activity: during the period

Table 11. **R&D output of Poland (PL) and the CSFR (CS) by industry Measured by patent activity**

| Industry/field of technology | Inventions [1] in 1982-88 | | | | Index of specialisation with reference to activity | | | |
| | Share in % [2] | | Share of CMEA in % | | worldwide [3] | | CMEA [4] | |
	PL	CS	PL	CS	PL	CS	PL	CS
Chemicals [5]	12	5	8	9	159	69	199	86
Production of plastics	6	1	20	7	92	9	230	196
Pharmaceuticals	2	4	1	8	29	83	27	76
Plastic products	2	3	4	16	80	112	113	15
Iron and steel	3	1	4	5	177	79	104	46
Foundries	1	1	2	6	60	81	46	61
Mechanical engineering	35	56	3	13	122	194	85	134
Agricultural machinery	2	3	2	12	158	343	58	125
Machine tools	5	54	4	7	164	123	94	70
Textile machinery	2	26	1	44	110	1628	30	446
M.f.food ind. packaging	0	0	0	2	14	26	11	158
M.f.rubber, plastic ind.	2	3	4	16	80	112	113	47
M.f.mining	3	0	17	5	1189	124	450	47
M.f.steel and allied industries	2	1	4	7	264	185	101	71
Construction machinery	1	1	2	5	104	80	63	49
Handling, lifting	7	3	7	6	315	108	180	62
Robotics	0	1	0	18	0	166	0	184
Gears, transmission equipment	3	5	4	19	98	172	108	190
Electrical engineering	11	8	4	8	53	37	106	75
Power generation	3	2	4	7	93	65	108	75
Telecommunication equip.	2	0	6	4	50	11	164	36
Consumer electronics	0	0	1	3	9	7	35	27
Office, EDP equipment	4	2	5	5	40	16	130	53
Motor vehicles	6	9	4	16	55	91	98	164
Air & space equipment	1	0	3	4	45	23	70	36
Precision instr., optics	18	19	3	9	98	103	89	95
All technologies	100	100	4	10	100	100	100	100

1. With patent application in at least two countries.
2. Because individual inventions may be relevant for more than one industry double counting occurs. The shares of industries may therefore add up to more than 100 per cent.
3. Share of industry/field of technology in worldwide inventions = 100.
4. Share of industry/field of technology in inventions originating from CMEA countries = 100.
5. If not mentioned as special field.

Source : IFO.

1982-1988, there were only 395 Polish inventions with patent application in at least two countries (against 5 037 in the former GDR, 2 068 in Hungary, and 1 033 in the CSFR). The index of specialisation, based on world innovation patterns, reveals that Polish R&D has concentrated more than the average worldwide on machinery for mining, handling and lifting, iron and steel, agriculture, and chemicals. The CSFR innovation system has focused on different areas, particularly in the engineering sector: textile machinery, gears and transmission equipment, robotics, and machinery for the rubber and plastics industry. Examination of the R&D specialisation profile in the light of an index based on CMEA innovation patterns shows that patent applications on western markets for both Polish and CSFR inventions in the general field of machinery were far more numerous than applications for inventions in the field of electronics and consumer durables (e.g. telecommunications, office and data processing equipment in the case of Poland; automobile industry in the case of the CSFR).

The patent statistics point to major weaknesses in the Polish innovation system which must be corrected during the transition process. They are:

— low overall efficiency, due to the lack of economic incentives to innovate (the "no carrot, no stick" economic system), insufficient infrastructural support for innovation (a financial system unable to manage industrial R&D risk properly, underdeveloped telecommunications, etc.), and inadequate organisation of the S&T system (excessive centralisation of research activities in national institutions, to the detriment of enterprise in-house research activities);

— a marked dualism that reflects the dual structure of trade (part of the R&D output does not meet world commercial standards) and the weight of defence-related research activities;

— a sectoral bias in the allocation of R&D resources that mirrors the distorted sectoral structure of production and employment (in particular, the modest role played by the consumer durable goods sectors as technology developers, adapters or purchasers).

These weaknesses have had two major consequences: the atrophy of world-class innovation capabilities in electronics and related fields and a low rate of diffusion of modern technologies in all industrial sectors. The latter phenomenon is not only attributable to the shortage of modern domestic or foreign equipment but also to ineffective channels for technology diffusion and insufficient absorptive capacity in user industries.

IV. Structural adjustment outlook: a medium term scenario

The integration of Polish industry into world markets will entail structural changes dependent on two sets of factors:

— The prices of production factors will reflect more and more the true opportunity cost of their use; this will change the "price-competitiveness" patterns within industry.

— The non-price factors of competitiveness will induce selection according to the relative capacity of enterprises to meet world standards of management, marketing, production techniques and product quality; this process will not be sectorally neutral.

The question for policy makers is whether these market-driven structural changes will more likely:

— consolidate and accentuate the current sectoral specialisation profile;

— shape a different sectoral profile; or

— affect the intra-sectoral more than the inter-sectoral distribution of industrial activities.

The point is not to choose a scenario and then frame policy so as to favour its realisation. There is no scenario that would lead, in all circumstances, to more vigorous economic growth. But given the point of departure and the international competitive situation, one may be regarded as the most probable for Polish industry. The following paragraphs advocate that the third scenario is more likely to emerge from market processes. It should be therefore taken as a frame of reference for formulating a strategy for industrial adjustment. A major practical implication is that industrial policy should focus on environment and selectivity at firm level rather than on sectoral development, although some sectoral programmes could be needed as a complement to this basic strategy (an idea to be elaborated in later sections of the report).

A. A narrow industrial adjustment path

At the outset of the transition period, Poland may seem to be in a delicate position. On the one hand, low domestic savings and a limited capacity to rejuvenate rapidly the industrial R&D system severely restrict the creation of comparative advantages in capital- and/or research-intensive industries. On the other hand, in labour-intensive sectors, competition from less developed market economies threatens to prevent Poland from exploiting fully the competitive advantage of very low wage costs and thereby transforming a transitional weakness into a source of capital accumulation for future development. (For a comparison with wages in European OECD countries, see Chart 1.12 in the Annex.) There would be a dead end if the existing distribution of industrial employment and production by classes of production factor intensity conformed to Polish production factor endowment. This is clearly not the case, and the reduction of this mismatch may constitute a sustainable, though narrow, adjustment path during the transition period.

Matching factor endowment and industrial specialisation means first breaking the ties between a rather highly qualified labour force and obsolete capital which have created an economy that is both capital- and labour-intensive (see Table 12), and has consequently very low total factor productivity.

In a market context, the qualification of labour cannot compensate for the inadequacy of the capital stock. Market mechanisms will first create a stronger link between technological obsolescence and economic obsolescence. Then, provided that the financial and labour markets function better, market mechanisms should ensure that allocation of new investment (both for replacement/modernisation and for capacity expansion) is justified by prospective returns.

It is difficult to know which activities might benefit from this rationalisation of production structures and therefore constitute the springboard for economic recovery. It is likely to be those that are skilled labour-intensive and have moderate capital and R&D requirements. Only a few sectors present all these features, but many include specific activities and enterprises which do.

B. Facing competition from low wage countries

Many developing countries have lower wages than Poland could maintain, even for a short period, without social unrest and/or an intolerable increase in the brain drain and emigration (see the worldwide comparison of wage levels in the textile industry in Table 1.6 in the Annex). And many newly industrialised countries enjoy highly competitive unit labour costs, thanks to the combination of moderate wages and high productivity. These countries have demonstrated their competitiveness on the world's most demanding markets in segments of a number of sectors. Table 13 shows these sectors classified according to factor intensities. Some important conclusions can be drawn:

Table 12. **Percentage distribution of manufacturing employment by degree of factor intensity and of competition from Low-Wage Countries (LWC), 1990**

Degree	LWC		Capital intensity		R&D intensity	
	Poland	CSFR	Poland	CSFR	Poland	CSFR
Very high	23.2	19.5	11.0	13.2	0.0	0.0
High	12.2	9.9	29.6	24.6	11.1	10.2
Medium	31.0	26.9	17.9	17.2	26.4	34.3
Low	15.7	15.7	32.3	38.6	62.5	55.5
Very low	17.9	28.0	9.2	6.4	0.0	0.0
Total	100.0	100.0	100.0	100.0	100.0	100.0
Number (thousands)	3 297	2 435	3 297	2 435	3 297	2 435

Sources : OECD, IFO.

Table 13. **Classification of industries according to factor intensity and degree of competition from Low-Wage Countries**

Intensity of		Degree of competition from Low-Wage Countries		
R&D	Capital	Low	Medium	High
Low	Low	Steel construction	Metal products	Jewellery, toys Pottery, china Metal articles Leather Footwear Clothing Furnitures
	Medium	Foundries Printing, publ.	Paper products	Wood products Textiles
	High	Pulp and paper	Non-ferrous metals Shipbuilding Glass Non-metal products Food products Oil refining Iron and steel	Tobacco
Medium	Low	Mechanical eng.		Rubber products Plastic products
	High	Motor vehicles Chemicals		
High	Low	Electrical mach. Air & space equip. Pharmaceuticals	Instruments	
	Medium			Electronic
	High			EDP equipment

1. Telecommunication equipment, consumer electronics, semi-conductors.
Sources: OECD, IFO.

65

— Low R&D intensity and high labour intensity do not automatically give a competitive edge to developing or newly industrialised countries. Important forward linkages (metal products) or a relatively high share of skilled labour (steel construction) can protect against low wage competition.

— High capital intensity does not protect against competition from low wage countries in all cases. If the forward linked branches are a domain of these countries (textiles) or if the availability of natural resources plays an important role (wood products and tobacco), capital intensification offers only limited protection.

— High R&D intensity does not offer absolute protection either. If technology transfer is easy, the production process not too complex, and skill requirements not high (as in the production of various electronics-based products), the competition from low wage countries may be very strong.

Table 12 shows the degree to which the current Polish industrial structure overlaps with the export structure of low wage countries. Polish industry appears to be more vulnerable to competition from low wage countries than the CSFR. Almost one-third of Polish industrial jobs are found in activities where low wage countries have demonstrated high competitiveness on western markets.

C. Polish industry's international competitive standing

To define further the conditions for Poland's successful integration into world markets, the current state of those markets must first be described, at least in broad terms. This means examining the position of Polish industry with respect both to low wage exporting countries and to highly developed market economies, especially EC countries. Table 14 offers a view of the situation.

The vulnerability of Polish industry to competitive pressures from low wage countries (LWC) can be assessed at a fairly disaggregated level on the basis of two indicators. The first is the degree of vulnerability to low wage competition (DOV). It shows the degree to which each industrial sector's exports are concentrated in product groups that LWC sell successfully in western European markets. Clothing, footwear, food products and tobacco, non-ferrous metals, and furniture exhibit above average exposure to LWC competition in western markets. The second indicator is the difference between DOVs for Poland and DOVs for the EC: it compares the vulnerability of Polish exporters to that of their EC competitors.

Table 14. **Polish industry in the context of global competition**

	Employees in 1 000	Cap. Int.	R&D Int.	LWC Int.	DOV %	DOV PO-EC[2]	Specialised in the EC[3]	Technological leaders[4]
Oil refining	33	HH	L	M	11.2	-0	ON, UK	
Food products	428	H	L	M	26.8	17	ON, OS, UK, F	
Tobacco	11	H	L	H	33.9	31	I, ON,F, OS	
Textiles	290	M	L	HH	32.1	12	OS, I	
Clothing	195	LL	L	HH	48.0	8	OS, I, UK	
Leather	41	L	L	HH	23.1	3	OS, I, F	
Footwear	88	L	L	HH	42.9	-1	I, OS, F	
Wood products	84	M	L	H	12.1	-5	OS	
Furnitures	80	L	L	HH	21.0	6	I	
Paper & pulp	27	HH	L	LL	3.5	2	UK	
Paper products	17	M	L	M	10.2	4	UK, ON, F	
Printing, publishing	35	M	L	L	10.1	5	ON, D	
Chemicals	166	HH	M	L	8.2	4	F, ON, OS	US, G
Pharmaceuticals	26	L	H	L	6.2	1	I, ON	US, EC
Rubber products	32	L	M	H	12.9	2	F, I	
Plastic products	47	L	M	H	10.4	-1	G	G
Pottery, china	23	L	L	H	17.7	4	I, O	
Glass	47	H	L	M	12.5	4	F, OS	
Non-metal products	135	H	L	M	16.9	7	OS, I	
Iron and steel	136	HH	L	M	10.6	4	I, ON, OS	J, G
Non-ferrous metals	58	H	L	M	23.9	15	ON, OS	
Foundries	50	M	L	L	5.4	1	G	G
Metal products	70	L	L	M	14.4	5	F	
Metal articles	69	L	L	H	17.0	7	G, OS	
Steel construction	35	LL	L	LL	4.2	2	F, I, ON	
Mechanical engineering	385	L	M	LL	4.2	1	G	G
Electrical engineering	118	L	H	LL	17.9	5	G, ON	J, G
Electronics[5]	115	M	H	H	19.9	6	ON, G, F, UK	J, US
Motor vehicles	241	H	M	L	5.7	2	G, F	G, J
Shipbuilding	35	H	L	M	8.2	-0	UK, ON, OS	
Air & space equipment	25	L	H	LL	2.5	0	UK, F	US, F, UK
Instruments, prof. goods	62	L	H	M	6.6	-1	G, UK	J
EDP equipment	20	H	H	H	15.5	4	F, I	J, US
Jewellery, toys, sports goods	73	LL	L	HH	50.1	20	F, UK, ON	
Total	3 297				20.0	11		

Cap.int. = capital intensity (Capital stock per employee, for details see Graph 9 in the annex).
R&D int. = R&D intensity according to OECD classification.
LWC int. = intensity of low wage competition from DCs and NICs (for details see Graph 10 in thennex).
1. Degree of vulnerability (DOV) of the exports to low wage competition; DOV is a weighted share of non-OECD imports in total OECD imports by product group (SITC 5-Digit); the weights correspond to the share of the product group in the exports of the country considered.
2. PO-EC = DOV for Polish exports minus DOV for EC exports.
3. Specialisation measured by the industry's share in total employment of manufacturing industry.
4. According to IFO patent statistics.
5. Telecommunication equipement, consumer electronics, semi-conductors.

HH = very high; H = high; M = medium; L = low; LL = very low.
ON = Other Northern EC (Denmark, Ireland, Benelux); OS = Other Southern EC (Greece, Portugal, Spain).

Sources : OECD; Eurostat; IFO; Polish Ministry of Industry and Trade (Promasz).

The position of Polish industry with respect to suppliers from highly developed economies can be determined by identifying the EC countries specialised in each industry and the world technological leaders in knowledge-intensive sectors. The situation is quite clear:

— In a free trade area such as the European Community, specialisation accurately reflects underlying comparative advantages. The EC countries specialised in industries where low wage costs do not constitute the dominant factor of competitiveness (with below average DOV) all enjoy production factor endowment that Poland cannot hope to emulate in the short to medium term. But Polish enterprises can envisage a niche strategy in the export and home market.

— Less advanced EC countries have an industrial specialisation profile which largely overlaps Poland's.

— Integration into world markets does not involve trade relationships alone. The Polish production structure must also be integrated into worldwide production and technological networks. In particular, massive technology transfers, either as foreign investment or in other forms, will be crucial during transition. Table 14 gives some indication of the countries most likely to be "technological partners for the transition".

When it entered the new economic era, Polish industry specialised in the production of textiles, leather and footwear, wood products, food processing, iron and steel, non-ferrous metals, metal products, and shipbuilding.

The three first sectors will encounter growing competition from low wage countries in both export and home markets, but the food industry may become a leading sector in Polish industrial redevelopment[9]. However, bottlenecks — including capital shortages and the delays inherent in modernising production technologies and adapting products to western tastes and styles — will impede expansion for some time. The major bottleneck, however, is constituted by trade barriers: in particular, the Association Agreement with the EC is more restrictive for agricultural and food products than for other "sensitive products" such as textiles, steel and coal. Despite the recent surge in exports of certain steel products, severe problems still confront the Polish iron and steel industry. They concern the environment, technological backwardness, and low energy efficiency, as well as the need to adjust domestic unit consumption of steel to far lower western standards (see Chart 1.11 in the Annex). Their solution will pro-

68

bably require a reduction in total capacity and specialisation in selected modernised segments of the industry. Finally, if supply factors justify specialisation in shipbuilding and steel construction, demand factors will for some time prevent Poland from taking full advantage of this strength. These sectors are highly dependent on the world investment climate. They are unlikely to expand in the current climate of lower OECD growth, and probably not before 1993.

D. Integrating into the international division of labour

Examination of Poland's international competitiveness, in terms of both supply and demand, shows that a restructuring process built on existing industrial specialisation would fail to create a solid basis for economic recovery. The efficiency of industrial targeting is uncertain in most circumstances, and such a policy would, in Poland even more than elsewhere, penalise good firms in non-targeted sectors and unduly favour bad firms in the chosen sectors.

More effective would be the integration of Polish industry into the intra-industrial division of labour in as many industries as possible, by building on its indisputable advantage in low-cost skilled labour and on local industrial traditions. Relying mainly on enterprise-level restructuring and initiative, which does not exclude sectoral initiatives in exceptional cases, this strategy would be the wisest for a number of reasons:

— Global competition between enterprises opens up opportunities for Polish enterprises to enter the world sourcing networks of dominant global players (e.g. transport equipment, electrical engineering or electronics). The free access to the EC market for many relevant products, granted by the Association Agreement, should facilitate the exploitation of such opportunities.

— If Poland eventually enters the EC, intra-industry specialisation resembles the intra-EC division of labour (intra-industry trade represents a large and growing share of total trade among EC countries).

— The integration of Polish industry into world markets will entail adjustment costs in other countries. The more its exports are sectorally diversified and geographically dispersed, the less will the adjustment process encounter policy obstacles.

E. The current adjustment bias

It is important to know whether recent industry trends are congruent with the desirable patterns of structural changes outlined above and whether the emerging market forces are already promoting the most promising type of structural adjustment, given the nature of Polish comparative advantages in the international competitive arena.

This does not appear to be the case. In the light of the recent relative performance of the different sectors, three indicators point to the presence of an adjustment bias:

— In the last two years, performance — production, export — has generally been better in heavy, energy-intensive sectors than in lighter industries.

— Exports have been concentrated more and more in certain product groups, especially metallurgical goods.

— If sectors are ranked according to their long-term competitiveness using the DRC (Domestic Resource Cost) method, and if the two extreme sets of sectors (each representing 10 per cent of total production value) are selected and their recent export performance compared, it is clear that the share of total exports of the most competitive sectors has decreased over the last two years, whereas that of the least competitive has increased over the same period.

The current economic depression is playing a role in the selection process, but it is also introducing distortions in the relative performances of firms which do not necessarily reflect their long-term economic viability[10]. A bias in the adjustment process is created by the combined effect of supply factors (immaturity of market mechanisms, distortions of incentives faced by the state-owned enterprises, and more generally the inertia of the inherited industrial structure) and transitional demand factors (affecting both the level and the structure of demand — see section II above). The bias is accentuated by the fact that environmental damages are not yet reflected in production costs; this raises a number of issues examined in later chapters.

Chapter 3

Removing obstacles
to structural adjustment

Since 1989, Poland's industrial enterprises have been subjected to extreme pressures. Individually, these could have stimulated positive changes, but their combined and cumulative impacts appears to have inhibited industrial restructuring and complicated the privatisation process. The unresponsiveness of industrial enterprises and structures jeopardises macroeconomic achievement. Microeconomic rigidities and disequilibria are rebounding on macroeconomic conditions.

The government's tight monetary and fiscal policies, designed to combat inflation, have reduced domestic demand more than expected, increased the cost of capital and inflated the state-owned enterprises' tax burden. The collapse of ex-CMEA trade made it necessary for many companies to change their product mix and improve their marketing skills overnight, at a time when their competitive standing on the domestic market was deteriorating due to the combined effect of trade liberalisation and real exchange rate appreciation.

Very strong incentives to privatise have not been matched by institutional and economic ability to support rapid privatisation on a large scale. As a result, few enterprises have succeeded in privatising; a vast majority have found themselves completely blocked in the attempt.

Supporting this argument is the following outline interpretation of the sequence of events in the state industrial sector over the last two years:

— Poland's industrial enterprises were subjected to a threefold shock, with massive changes in relative prices (energy prices, in particular soaring), markets (both domestic and ex-CMEA) shrinking, and pressure from imports.

— Initially, enterprises responded indecisively, this giving rise to a feeling of disquiet about the future, which was fuelled in particular by speculation about government intentions regarding privatisation and, more generally, industrial policy. The outcome was that wage claims moderated, causing real wages to fall. This, coupled with the consequences of hyperinflation (appreciation of the value of stocks and reduction in the burden of debt), contributed to a temporary surge in profits and gave many enterprises the impression that they could afford "wait and see". Those most affected by the collapse of certain markets tended to rely on hypothetical government measures, taking the view that the scale of their problems required solutions outside their means and, also, that the authorities had a historical responsibilities towards them.

— The temporary improvement in the financial situation was not, therefore, used by firms to implement the reforms that the situation warranted. It also came too soon for the government to be able to take advantage of it in the context of its privatisation policy, then still at the preparation stage. The government was not able of countering the "wait and see" attitude of firms with measures that might have prompted them to adopt more positive survival strategies.

— With no let-up in the pressure to adjust, the business situation very quickly deteriorated and the cost of inaction mounted. Thus in the space of few months, the level of debt, which had been temporarily reduced, again reached record levels. At the same time, the privatisation programme had taken shape, but few enterprises were in a position to take advantage of the possibilities it offered. The incentives introduced in order to encourage the development of the private sector, which consisted of prompting firms to volunteer by concentrating the bulk of tax pressure on state-owned firms, proved ill-suited to a task for which they had not been designed, i.e. promoting prior industrial restructuring.

— Many firms adopted the short-term survival strategy allowed by the government reluctance to apply the financial disciplines originally included in its Economic Transformation Programme. In particular they accumulated debt — with government in the shape of unpaid tax and with suppliers in the shape of inter-enterprise credit — and stopped investing. In some cases, even, the existence of a tax on excessive wage increases did not deter them from accelerating the devaluation of their assets to the advantages of wages. The newly created commercial banks, too, were disinclined to trigger the failure of such enterprises, no doubt gambling on future individual rescue operations by the government, or an overall solution to the debt problem. In many cases they were willing to capitalise the interest, and sometimes even to grant additional loans to insolvent clients. Their balance sheets were burdened by bad debts which weakened their capacity to back viable restructuring projects.

— For it was a fact that not all state-owned enterprises were managed on the basis of this "distress" strategy. A number of them, both the management and the workers' councils fairly soon realised what measures were needed. Not soon enough, however, for their ability to implement them not to be seriously jeopardised by the increasingly pervasive crisis in the state sector. Many such enterprises were prevented from acting, tied up as they were in the network of inter-enterprise credits, crippled with taxes, poorly supported by a weakened and inexperienced banking system, and deprived of access to international funds.

— This spread of the crisis in the state industrial sector made the threat of bankruptcy less and less credible, enterprises being aware of the government concern to avoid a whole series of closures.

Even if it may be hoped that the depression has now bottomed out (industrial output recently showed an upturn for the first time for two years), firms are going to emerge from these two years of crisis in a weakened state. The main factors behind the scenario just described have to be neutralised before a strong and lasting recovery can take place. These will be analysed in greater detail in the rest of the chapter

I.   Structural adjustment issues

A. *The slow pace of privatisation*

Privatisation has proved to be a very slow and difficult process. Two simple figures demonstrate how disappointing the privatisation record is: according to official sources, privatisation proceedings in 1991 amounted to only 2 500 billions zlotys, when 15 000 billions were expected. The details of the progress of privatisation were reported in Chapter 1. Suffice it to say here that expectations about privatisation have not been met, for two major reasons.

First, for political reasons, it has proved difficult for the government to allow state-owned enterprises to go bankrupt, despite some progress in tightening the bankruptcy law. Second, there is a scarcity of resources to privatise those state-owned enterprises which, according to reports of foreign consultants and other information, are generally believed to be potentially competitive at world prices despite their current financial insolvency. There are now some Polish citizens who have substantial wealth, but generally they are insufficient in number to absorb anywhere near the large number of Polish state-owned enterprises eligible for privatisation. It should be remembered that even before the Second World War, large Polish industry was principally owned by the government — it is estimated that 70 per cent of large firms were state-owned in the 1930's. Therefore, there is little legacy in Poland of large-scale capitalists. Wealthy Polish citizens have also preferred to invest in commerce and non-production related services rather than in industry, because of the "second economy syndrome" (preference for low exposure of investment, rapid turnover of the capital, opportunities of tax evasion, etc.), but also because investment in manufacturing is seldom attractive in the current economic environment.

Moreover, the inflow of foreign resources into Poland has been limited. As indicated in Chapter 1, although it is estimated that more than two thousand joint ventures have been established, many are in non-manufacturing activities and most are small (around 70 employees on average). Major foreign buy-outs of Polish enterprises have been rare (and it is probably safe to say that by mid-1992 there were no more than 20 major foreign buy-outs of Polish enterprises).

It may be added that whereas all foreign loans and grants committed to Poland are estimated by the Polish government to amount to as much as $10 billion ($5 billion in the form of lines of credit from various governments), only a very small portion of that amount is designated for restructuring Polish industry. The main loan to Poland for industrial restructuring (on the premise that some restructuring is necessary to further privatisation) is from the World Bank. It totals $280 million. Of that amount, the component designated for restructuring industry — that is, for financing the direct foreign exchange cost of physical improvements to production, technology transfer, and so forth — is approximately $140 million, to be disbursed over six years (see Table 15).

Yet $140 million can realistically restructure only a very few firms. Even if the cost of restructuring a representative firm is only $1 million, only 140 firms can be restructured with World Bank assistance, out of a total number of state-owned enterprises in the industrial sector of about 7 000, including almost 3 000 in the manufacturing/mining sector. Of that total number of state-owned enterprises, say, only half or even a third are

Table 15.   **Foreign assistance to Poland**

**Geographic distribution of aid and assistance
to Central and Eastern European countries, 31.12.1990**
In percent

Country	Bilateral assistance by members of G-24 and the EC	Assistance by multilateral organisations
Poland	40.6	50.9
Hungary	27.2	30.5
CSFR	5.2	9.7
Romania	2.1	3.1
Bulgaria	1.1	5.8
Unallocated	23.8	-
Total	100.0	100.0

Source : Commission of the European Communities, *Progress report on G-24 assistance to Central and Eastern Europe,* 30 January 1991.

Major sources of aid to Poland
Loans over the period 1990-1993; $ million

IMF stabilisation funds	1 000
World Bank	2 500
European Investment Bank	1 090
Bilateral credits	5 000
of which (Germany)	(1 160)
(Japan)	(850)
(France)	(700)
(United States)	(600)
(Italy)	(500)
(Korea)	(450)

Sources: Polish official sources; UNIDO; World Bank.

Some major World Bank assistance programmes
$ million

Privatisation and restructuring	280
Export promotion	260
Agro-industry development	100
Rail transport modernisation	150
Natural gas investment	600
Import of essential goods and benefits and training to unemployed	300

Source: World Bank.

viable in the long run. That still leaves too little money to restructure even the most promising firms, which the government numbers at a minimum at some 800 to 1 000 (the number of enterprises eligible for mass privatisation, and hence, viable in the long term). Moreover, the estimate of $1 million per firm for restructuring is very low. In the case of one average company in the light industry sector, for example, the short-run costs of the necessary capital equipment alone were estimated by a foreign consulting firm to be $1.5 million. In the case of the big "dinosaurs" (in mining, heavy industry, mechanical industry, chemicals, etc.) the "unit restructuring cost" can easily reach $50 million, as the German experience shows.

B. The precarious situation of state-owned enterprises

Given a shortage of private buyers and a reluctance on the government's part to liquidate obviously unviable enterprises, privatisation has progressed only slowly, and Poland's state-owned enterprises have been left in a precarious state. Many of them are highly indebted but neither entirely bankrupt nor in a position to compete internationnaly. They require restructuring — in terms of modernisation of some of their production technology, their product offering, management system, finance, and marketing — but from past trends of foreign capital inflow, they cannot expect foreign resources to help them through the crisis that now threatens their very existence as productive enterprises.

1. High indebtedness

In Poland, all debts, whether to the government (tax authorities, social security), the banks, or other firms, are subject to penalty interest rates if they fall into arrears and are not paid by the date contracted. For example, the banking system penalises arrears at almost twice the loan interest rate.

Many Polish state-owned enterprises have fallen deeply into debt as a consequence of not adjusting to changes in relative prices, to the abrupt decline in demand from ex-CMEA countries, and to a sharp rise in imports. Unlike firms in most countries, they have fixed tax obligations that are unrelated to their profitability (the tax on assets, called *dividenda*, which, incidentally, penalises the most modern firms). Like firms everywhere, Polish enterprises also borrowed to cover operating costs; in the case of the textile industry, for instance, they borrowed to import their major raw material, cotton. Operating costs also rose steeply as the government ceased subsidizing the price of energy inputs.

During the opening phase of the transition, the very high inflation rate, a credit crunch, and the liberalisation of bank interest rates (the object of governement financial policy was to make real interest rates positive), resulted in nominal interest rates on the order of 100 - 200 per cent per annum, applied monthly. For exemple in April 1990, the monthly interest rate was 8 per cent, a figure which exceeded the inflation rate by 5.7 per cent. When sales plummetted due to a decline in foreign and especially domestic demand, indebtedness increased. Firms were unable to meet their financial obligations and interest rate penalties on loans in arrear were activated. Therefore, real and effective interest rates, including penalties, rose even further.

The number of enterprises unable to meet their financial obligations soared in 1991. Of the 1 658 enterprises supervised by the Ministry of Industry and Trade:

— more than 750 state-owned enterprises were behind in their payment obligations (tax and social security) to the State in July 1991, compared to 350 in January of the same year;

— also in July 1991, more than 450 enterprises were not paying the obligatory dividend (*dividenda*) to the Treasury, compared with only 165 in December 1990;

— more than 170 industrial enterprises had lost their creditworthiness (according to bank evaluations) as of May 1991 and were not paying their obligations to other firms; and

— nearly 250 industrial enterprises were operating at a loss in April 1991, compared to only 65 at the end of 1990.

The situation did not improve in the latter part of the year. At the end of November 1991, around 40 per cent of state-owned enterprises reported losses. Among those supervised by the Ministry of Industry and Trade, 718 were in a desperate or difficult financial position; 250 firms employing more than 500 people were technically bankrupt while another 300 were expected to fail in the near future.

If a growing number of enterprises fail to pay, the government will have also accumulate an enormous debt vis-à-vis enterprises in the armaments industry, public utilities and many other sectors. At the end of 1991, it was officially announced that the amount of this debt has not yet been established but could vary from 20 trillion zlotys to over 40 trillion zlotys (i.e. from $2 billion to over $4 billion). This accelerates the "vicious circle of indebtedness".

Many enterprises are currently suffering from major liquidity and profitability crises arising from lack of sales and the spiralling costs of penalty
interest rate charges on debt obligations. Restrictions on working capital
result, and they, in turn, have the following effects:

— Purchases of production inputs are driven by what can be afforded
   rather than what should be bought. This will invariably interrupt
   supply and reduce overall quality.

— Routine maintenance and replacement of spare parts are sacrificed, thereby raising production costs and threatening the continuity of production.

— Product diversification and sales expansion cannot be financed.

— Consumer and supplier confidence are shaken. A shortage of working capital causes a firm to lose its customer base. In turn, this
   reduces the profitability and viability of the enterprise still further,
   which makes the vicious circle of indebtedness worse.

— "Capital consumption" (selling equipment for very low prices and
   even scrapping valuable equipment) is encouraged.

2. *Deterioration of "price-competitiveness"*

Inflation in Poland, estimated to be running at 3-4 per cent per month,
has quickly changed from being demand-driven (typical of "shortage" economies under communist rule) to cost-driven (typical of economies in the
process of stabilization). High real interest rates are only one of a number
of factors that have begun to make Poland a "high cost economy". Other
factors pushing up costs include high costs of mass-layoffs (6 months salary
has to be paid, instead of 3 months in the case of individual dismissal), the
low level of services usually provided by government to business (information, telecommunications, training, overseas promotion), and an underdeveloped retail as well as wholesale distribution system.

It is noteworthy that in 1989 the real wage fell by about 50 per cent.
This does not necessarily mean that the living standard of workers declined
by half — queues, for example, disappeared. The real wage increased in
1990, but wages and incomes generally remained depressed. In 1990 real
per capita income was estimated to be only 93.6 per cent of its 1980 level.
The share of wages in the production costs of state-owned enterprises fell
slightly from the last quarter of 1990 over that of 1989 from 15.5 per cent to
12.1 per cent. Real wages are estimated to have fallen in the last 24 months

78

by at least one-third, but unit labor costs in dollar terms have increased since January 1990 due to poor productivity performance.

Nevertheless, extremely low real wages (denominated in dollars), are proving to be an insufficient competitive advantage for many Polish sectors, including some labour-intensive activities which are now under more direct competitive pressure from developing and newly industrialised countries (see Chapter 2). The rise in other costs makes it harder for firms in Poland to compete in export markets or against competitive imports. This is especially the case since many foreign competitors in the Polish market and overseas operate with lower capital costs and in many cases more public support than Polish state-owned enterprises now do.

3. Weak "non-price competitiveness"

Whatever problems Polish enterprise confronts related to production costs, it faces severe problems related to its products as well. In a wide variety of industries, Poland's products are judged by consumers in non-CMEA markets to be of low quality or incorrect specifications compared with those supplied by foreign competitors. This is largely due to the previous absence of foreign competition. To a lesser degree, it is due to the former income distribution of Polish consumers. Although the pattern was less egalitarian than in any other communist country, it did not favour production of the differentiated products that are more in demand in export markets and now increasingly in Poland.

High quality products produced in Poland were often earmarked for the military, and military expenditures, which were at a relatively high level by world standards (see Chart 1.3 in the Annex), have been cut sharply. Moreover, high quality products were commercialised in a way that did not permit the enterprises to develop marketing know-how that they could now apply readily: high quality products were often produced exclusively for export (especially in the textile, clothing and leather industries) through monopolistic state-owned foreign trade organisations (FTOs); on the domestic market, they were sold through the informal channels of the second economy.

A firm's product mix and product quality cannot be changed overnight. Product transformation takes time and money. It requires management co-ordination, investment in new equipment, and, above all, better marketing and distribution. The conversion of production from military to civilian use also requires considerable effort. However, imports have been rapidly liberalised and the accompanying massive depreciation could not help meeting *qualitatively* the challenge. As a share of domestic consumption of industrial goods, imports accounted for 12.7 per cent in 1985 and 18.3 per cent in 1990. As a share of total imports, consumer goods rose from 18.8 per cent in 1990 to 31.6 per cent during the first eight months of 1991.

Increased imports can be expected to satisfy pent-up consumer demand and subject Polish industry to a much needed dose of competition. In the long term, this can only be healthy. In the short term, it may also temper the price increases that financially strapped and/or monopolistic domestic firms might otherwise introduce. But because the quality and mix of a firm's products cannot be altered quickly, import liberalisation has probably contributed in the short run to the financial insolvency of a large number of private industrial SMEs and, more generally, to the depressed state of Polish industry.

C. Negative externalities of state-owned enterprises on private firms

In a study of Poland's private manufacturing sector undertaken by the World Bank, some 3 000 private manufacturing SMEs were provisionally identified in early 1991. However, it was later found that some 1 500 had already ceased operation. A sample of 120 companies were selected, but by the time interviews began, one-third had failed and another third were in the process of doing so.

The World Bank singled out two major reasons for the high failure rate. First, many had been established with certain expectations about foreign competition. When the government liberalised imports in the second half of 1990, these SMEs did not have time to adjust to more intense foreign competition. Second, many relied on demand for their products from state-owned enterprises. As these began to suffer from declining demand and rising debt, a domino effect bankrupted the SMEs that were dependent on them. Additional reasons for failure include: high cost of capital, shrinking demand from Polish consumers, lack of management and marketing skills, and the inefficient and costly distribution system.

D. The crux of the problem

To summarise, state-owned enterprises in Poland's industrial sector fall into two general categories: on the one hand, firms that appear to be non-viable in the long run and require an immediate plan to liquidate them; and, on the other, long-run viable firms that are destined for privatisation but have not yet been transformed. Some of the latter may not wish to be privatised, some appear eager to do so, and some wish to be privatised if they are given a say in the choice of their new owner. These "orphans" also require an immediate solution because they are being crushed by their indebtedness. In Poland, financial insolvency no longer bears much systematic relationship to fundamental long-run competitive capability.

There are two possible outcomes, both undesirable, unless something decisive is done soon to revive the promising state-owned enterprises. One is that they fail despite their potential, thus making fewer firms available for privatisation in the long run. As a consequence, there will also probably be fewer private industrial SMEs in the near future, because the evidence suggests that many of the new private industrial enterprises that have emerged since 1989 depend on the demand of state-owned enterprises for their survival. Another outcome is that their value will depreciate to the point where they become cheap enough to attract a buyer. But "fire sales" are politically unpopular and socially destabilizing.

Even if foreign investors begin to arrive in Poland in greater numbers than in the past two years, which is highly desirable, the experiences of those late-industrialising countries that have received large inflows of foreign capital suggest that investment from abroad typically amounts to only a small share of total capital formation. Economic development has been financed overwhelmingly by domestic savings. Moreover, the arrival of foreign capital tends to lag rather than lead industrial development. It can accelerate industrial growth, but it usually does not trigger it.

In short, privatisation will not necessarily solve all the problems of Polish industry. At a minimum, all firms will need outside help in the form of training and advisory services. Privatisation is proving to be a long, drawn-out process. The government must not only make greater efforts to achieve this goal in the future, it must also decide how to deal with both viable and non-viable state-owned enterprises in the interim.

II.   Major obstacles to industrial restructuring

Industrial restructuring faces major obstacles and unless they are taken into consideration, the chances of formulating a realistic industrial policy are slim.

A. The macroeconomic constraints

Underlying structural factors such as those that prevent enterprises from curbing costs and raising efficiency, tend to keep inflationary pressures strongly entrenched. So long as they are not significantly weakened, industrial restructuring is unlikely to beneficit from more accomodating macroeconomic policies.

As emphasised in the recent *OECD Economic Survey*[1], the Polish government has little room to manoeuvre if it wants to achieve three main objectives:

— *Control over the budget.* The deficit should not surpass 5 per cent of GDP (it was 3.8 per cent in 1991). Given the characteristics of the Polish economy (an inadequate savings rate and underdevelopment of financial markets), this percentage should be seen as a maximum if a series of undesirable consequences are to be avoided. These include: the crowding out of credit to productive enterprises, increased foreign debt, and weakened government credibility vis-à-vis both domestic agents and potential foreign investors.

— *Control over inflation.* The government's objective is to reduce inflation rate to 36.5 per cent in 1992, as high inflation involves unsustainable costs. In an inflationary environment, high interest rates reduce the effective maturity of debt and create serious roll over problems, speculative behaviour is encouraged and financial markets are distorted. The goal will be difficult to achieve, in view of the mandated increases in energy prices.

— *Avoiding an over-valuation of the zloty.* Initially, the stabilisation programme established a "fixed nominal exchange rate" policy. The inherent danger of an over-valuation of the zloty — detrimental to the competitiveness of Polish enterprises — has led government to move to an explicit "crawling peg" policy, with a monthly depreciation of the exchange rate.

Tight monetary policy will remain the main macroeconomic tool for combatting inflation. Given the requirements imposed by the financing of a growing budget deficit, it is likely that such policy will continue to restrict severely the total amount of credit that banks can supply to enterprises.

B. Delay in building an efficient financial system

Inefficiencies in credit allocation aggravate the consequences of tight monetary policy. It is worth stressing again that Poland is only developing slowly a market-oriented financial system. Thus, assumptions about how an economy works in the presence of an efficient capital market cannot be presumed to apply. It is necessary to consider whether policies that take a smoothly operating capital market for granted are likely to succeed under less favourable conditions.

Newly established Polish commercial banks are still far from behaving like energetic and efficient financial intermediaries for industrial restructuring. They are just learning to understand industrial risk assessment, project appraisal, financial engineering and services, etc. Their behaviour is also influenced by the uncertainties surrounding government plans to tackle the overall debt problem. Finally, their present situation is fragile, due to the recent sharp increase in the share of non-performing assets in their portfolios.

As a consequence, many potentially productive enterprises are starved of the funds needed for restructuring, while some scarce credit resources are still being wasted on non-viable firms. Should credit allocation not improve rapidly, irreversible damage could be done to the industrial structure.

C. Inadequate incentive structure

Improvement of credit allocation carries few benefits if enterprises do not have the incentives to use financial resources efficiently. At present, the incentive structure for state-owned entreprises is confusing. There are strong incentives to privatise but inadequate incentives to restructure prior to privatisation. This would not be a problem if the only bottleneck in the privatisation process was the attitude of enterprise management and workers' councils. But there are others. The institutional capability to handle the privatisation process speedily is limited; more important still, the balance sheets of the state-owned enterprises have deteriorated, thus reducing dramatically the number of firms eligible for privatisation through transformation or liquidation under Article 37.

To achieve rapid progress in privatisation while maintaining its voluntary character, management and workers must be given good reasons not to exert their *veto* rights. Shares offered on concessional terms and tax instruments have been used for this purpose. Privatisation allows enterprises to escape from two taxes: the special tax on assets (*dividenda*) and the tax on excessive wages (*popiwek*). A close link has therefore been created between the incentive structure, which must be stable, and the budgetary and wage policy, which are influenced by short-term developments. The link with the wage policy is problematic, since there is a danger that privatisation will be accompanied by exaggerated expectations of high wage increases. The link with budgetary policy may be even more dangerous. Pending reform of the tax system, and given the current precarity of the budget situation, the concentration of tax pressures on state-owned enterprises may become an incentive to privatise that weakens the capacity to fulfil the requirements for privatisation.

The special tax on assets levied on state-owned enterprises (*dividenda*) is also intended to be instrumental in enforcing hard budget constraints; failure to pay the tax constitutes a criterion for insolvency and allows the founding ministry to initiate liquidation proceedings. A tight budget constraint enforced through the threat of bankruptcy and increased foreign competition were the two incentives introduced by the Economic Transformation Programme to induce efficient behaviour on the part of state-owned enterprises, pending their privatisation. In reality, the inadequacy of the bankruptcy law (see above) and the political reluctance to enforce it have weakened the role that the threat of bankruptcy can play as an incentive for enterprises to adapt to the new market environment. Moreover, in the absence of a credible budget constraint, the effect of other incentives is distorted. For example, the tax on excessive wage increases has become more and more an important source of budget revenue for the State and less and less an encouragement to privatise or to exert wage discipline.

D. Lack of an inter-enterprise network infrastructure

Many information links among firms have been broken as a result of the dismantling of the centrally planned economy. One example is the wholesale trading system. This makes flows of information more difficult at a time when the entire economy is changing radically and accurate information, particularly with respect to privatisation policy, is at a premium. The situation presents an obstacle to industrial restructuring to the extent that it impedes "technology transfer", broadly defined, among firms and makes supplier relations, sub-contracting, and vertical disintegration more difficult. The underdevelopment of the professional service sector aggravates the situation.

E. The slow "marketisation" of the labour market

Poland's product markets have "marketised" rapidly; firms now act relatively autonomously and their prices, major costs, and investment decisions are no longer determined by a central plan. The "marketisation" of Poland's capital and labour markets, however, has progressed much more slowly. In many firms, labour is still a fixed rather than a variable input, although this is also true to some extent of the labour market in many OECD countries, particularly Japan. Moreover, it is relatively expensive for a company to terminate employment: severance pay and pensions carry high fixed costs.

In 1982, the government re-established workers' councils in most major state-owned enterprises in an attempt to make Polish managers in the public sector more responsive. In many companies, these workers' councils now have considerable say in strategic and operational decisions. They may also appoint the managing director and determine his salary level and conditions of promotion. One of the objectives of privatisation is to reduce the power of these workers' councils, which do not exist in private firms.

Redundancy is the major obstacle to industrial restructuring presented by a "non marketised" labour market. It is difficult for practical reasons to terminate the employment of employees of long standing, despite the fact that many enterprises operate under conditions of severe "feather-bedding" or "overmanning" and hence, have low productivity. Feather-bedding may not apply so much to direct production workers as to those engaged in providing social services to fellow employee — child care, health care, and so forth.

As noted earlier, Poland's tax on wage increases (*popiwek*) is designed to curb inflation and, at the same time, to incite workers to privatise, since privatised firms are not subject to *popiwek*. In 1990, the allowable wage increase was set at 30 per cent of the inflation rate in January, 20 per cent in February, March, and April, and 60 per cent during the rest of the year (except in July, when it was set to unity). State-owned enterprises were liable for tax penalties of 200-500 per cent on any cumulative increase above these ceilings.

Unfortunately, one consequence for over-pressured, "orphaned" state-owned enterprises awaiting privatisation is the increasing difficulty of motivating and rewarding workers. While *popiwek* may be necessary to stem inflation and to further the cause of privatisation, measures are needed to convince workers that they can expect benefits from increases in productivity and in the value of their firm.

Since 1989, many Polish state-owned enterprises have been labelled "worker-managed" because workers' councils have exercised decision-making power. This does not necessarily mean that they are poorly run, although more often than not the councils appear to have advocated higher wages and employee benefits rather than restructuring. Additionally, workers' councils might be a basis on which to build an enterprise-based system of collective bargaining, which could play a useful role in the restructuring process, especially when it is particularly painful.

In any case, the question of worker-managed firms is politically sensitive. Any policy to promote industrial restructuring must take the slow marketisation of the labour market into account and attempt to build on the best-run firms with the greatest future potential, whatever their type.

F. Scarce human resources to manage industrial restructuring

Policies to promote industrial restructuring are only as good as the human capital available to implement them in the administration and enterprises, but there is a shortage of experienced personnel.

Government bureaucracies and state-owned enterprises managements are no longer controlled by those people who reigned under communist rule; the *nomenklatura* have largely retired or gone into the private sector. This has left a hiatus in the public sector that will be filled only slowly.

The problem is not so much a shortage of well-educated people; indeed, as economic activity has declined, their numbers have not decreased. Although the bureaucracies and enterprises must compete with the burgeoning private sector (particularly new private banks), the economic depression seems to have created a "buyer's market", and the supply of well-educated people increasingly outstrips demand.

The problem, instead, is a shortage of experienced people with specific training, and limited funds for training them. Due to the high priority placed on privatisation, other activities within the government have necessarily been sacrificed. For example, seven times more assistance from the budget and international lending agencies is being directed to the Ministry of Ownership Changes, which is responsible for privatisation, than to the Ministry of Industry and Trade, which is responsible for restructuring.

In the enterprises, there is believed to be a significant shortage of business leaders equipped or accustomed to managing firms under competitive market conditions. There is also a great shortage of managers with expertise in marketing and distribution, since under a command economy little attention was paid to these functions. While there is probably no shortage of accountants with bookkeeping skills, there is a severe shortage of accountants capable of helping firms manage cost-effectively.

These skill shortages can be surmounted with investments in training and technology transfer, but this will take time.

G. The impoverishment of the science and technology (S&T) infrastructure

Before 1989, Poland spent relatively little on either R&D or improving manufacturing techniques, including outlays for mechanisation and automation. Outlays for improving manufacturing techniques as a percentage of output sold was 0.53 per cent in 1987, 0.65 per cent in 1988, and 0.37 per cent in 1989. Expenses for all forms of "technical progress", including R&D (performed in the Polish Academy of Sciences, colleges and universities, scientific research institutes, and central laboratories in enterprises) were 1.39 per cent of sales value in 1988 and 0.79 per cent in 1989 (see Table 16). For comparison, in many OECD countries, R&D expenses alone represent more than 2 per cent of the value of manufacturing output.

After 1989, Poland began to reorganise its S&T infrastructure. The already meagre investments in technical applications and R&D were cut further in the budget squeeze. Although investments in S&T by state-owned enterprises rose as a share of sales, this was due to a decline in sales rather than to an increase in absolute expenditures, which tended to fall. Cutbacks in S&T, particularly applied technical investments, constitute a barrier to restructuring because they reduce the ability to disseminate better technology widely. In the long run, Poland's competitiveness will depend on rebuilding a solid technology support system.

H. Barriers to Polish exports

All the obstacles to industrial restructuring discussed above act as domestic barriers to the expansion of Polish exports. But there exist foreign barriers as well, and they markedly affect certain sectors in which Poland might hope to demonstrate long-term comparative advantages.

Table 16. **Expenses for technical progress**
State-owned enterprises

| Sector | As % of sales | | | Total expenses 1990 | |
	1988	1989	1990	Value 10⁹ zl.	Share %
Total industry	1.39	0.79	0.86	4 349	100.0
Energy	0.99	0.50	0.31	286	6.6
Coal	1.57	1.19	0.80	184	4.2
Fuel	0.42	0.14	0.15	61	1.4
Power	1.01	0.28	0.15	42	1.0
Metallurgy	0.57	0.51	0.29	212	4.9
Iron and steel	0.39	0.24	0.24	110	2.5
Non-ferrous metals	0.82	0.96	0.36	101	2.3
Engineering	3.02	1.61	1.52	2 016	46.4
Metal products	1.23	0.81	0.53	133	3.1
Machinery, non-electrical	2.60	1.51	1.39	522	12.0
Precision instruments	1.32	2.51	2.71	171	3.9
Transport equipment	3.36	2.03	1.89	703	16.2
Electrical and electronics	4.38	1.69	1.89	487	11.2
Chemicals	1.23	0.68	1.18	634	14.6
Mineral products	0.97	0.86	0.87	177	4.1
Building materials	0.63	0.47	0.43	63	1.4
Glass	2.37	2.31	2.10	86	2.0
Earthenware/ceramics	0.62	0.70	1.75	28	0.7
Wood and paper	1.13	0.47	0.78	186	4.3
Wood	1.18	0.53	0.92	147	3.4
Paper	1.00	0.30	0.51	39	0.9
Light industry	0.40	0.23	0.35	136	3.1
Textiles	0.56	0.33	0.39	82	1.9
Clothing	0.16	0.15	0.29	27	0.6
Leather	0.27	0.09	0.31	28	0.6
Food industry	0.29	0.28	0.45	447	10.3
Other manufacturing	0.98	0.33	2.50	250	5.7

Source : Polish Ministry of Industry and Trade (Promasz).

moderately successful (see the recent *OECD Economic Survey*[1]). The most significant improvement in market access has been for the European Community.

Important barriers remain. In the case of the Association Agreement with the European Community, the GSP (from which steel and coal are excluded) is limited by contingents and quotas, and the suspension of quantitative restrictions is in many cases conditional on a lack of "difficulties" in EC Member countries, particularly in the area of textiles. Polish agricultural products face high barriers in all OECD countries (the OECD Secretariat estimates the *ad valorem* equivalent at 100 per cent).

III. Building on strengths

While Poland suffers from major barriers to industrial restructuring, it also exhibits considerable strengths on which to restructure. It would be misleading to paint a rosy picture, but at the same time it is unwarranted to portray the outlook as altogether bleak. In structural terms, Poland has some great advantages: it has a relatively large domestic market, with a population of almost 40 million people; its population is relatively well-educated and without politically divisive regional loyalties; some of its infrastructure in big cities (and transportation between certain big cities) is fairly modern; it is well endowed with raw materials; it has some promising state-owned enterprises, whose long-run viability appears encouraging; and it is possibly the largest agricultural region in Europe, with the potential for agriculture to serve as a springboard for industrial development.

In the following discussion of Poland's strengths, attention is restricted to education and the quality of some enterprises.

A. Educational attainments

In comparing Poland's educational attainments to those of other countries (see Table 17), it is important to differentiate levels of education and peer groups. In 1987, Poland's primary education was more or less on a par with that of OECD countries and with what the World Bank calls "upper-middle income" countries (say, Republic of Korea, Argentina, Hungary, and Romania). In secondary education, Poland was behind the OECD group but ahead of upper-middle income countries. In tertiary (university) education, Poland was well behind the OECD group and on a par only

Table 17. **Poland's educational attainments**
Percentage of age group enrolled in education

	Primary		Secondary		Tertiary	
	1965	1987	1965	1987	1965	1987
Poland	104	101	69	80	18	18
Upper-Middle Income [1]	92	104	32	67	7	20
OECD	104	103	63	94	21	39

1. A weighted average of South Africa, Algeria, Hungary, Uruguay, Argentina, Yugoslavia, Gabon, Venezuela, Trinidad and Tobago, Republic of Korea, Portugal, Greece, Oman, Libya, Iran, Iraq, and Romania.

Source : World Bank.

with the upper-middle income countries. Table 17 also indicates that in comparative terms, Poland has lost ground since 1965.

These comparisons are useful because educational requirements tend to vary across industries and, if one regards education as a competitive asset, they suggest the appropriate peer group for Poland to use as a point of reference in particular industries. The appropriate peer group is not always the OECD countries.

The quality of education, of course, varies across countries. In primary education, Poland has a relatively low ratio of pupils to teachers and high quality. Poland's educated elite also demonstrates high quality because it is quite "internationalised": a fairly sizeable number of educated Poles have worked or studied in the West, if only for short periods. Because of the large number of Poles who have migrated to the West, there is a constant flow of physical and human capital between Poland and the rest of the world. This "cosmopolitanism" is a strong point because it facilitates trade, technology transfer, and the possibility of "reverse brain drain".

B. The quality of many enterprises

From expert studies and plant visits, it appears impossible to generalise about the quality of state-owned enterprises by industry: most industries have promising and unpromising firms. Moreover, as discussed earlier, the present financial situation of an enterprise cannot serve as a reliable indicator of long-term viability and profitability (i.e. expected return on investment). Finally, in some firms, high profits reflect monopoly power rather than competitive capabilities. One must look at other factors besides current financial performances to evaluate the quality of state-owned enterprises, and this is one reason why assessing their viability for purposes of privatisation has taken a long time.

Industry data in the form of "domestic resource cost" (DRC) calculations can be used to obtain a first order approximation of the average cost-competitiveness of Polish enterprises in the absence of subsidies. Bearing in mind some severe estimation problems and under generally optimistic assumptions, the results suggest that in terms of cost, a large number of Polish industries are competitive at world prices. Generally a DRC of 1.0 implies that the value added of an industry is the same at world and domestic prices. On certain assumptions this can be taken as a dividing line between those industries that should be encouraged to expand and those that should contract or cease operations. However, if the exchange rate is judged to have been overvalued in the base period, say, by 50 per cent, then the cutoff should be DRCs with a value of 1.5 rather than 1.0. For all industries in Poland, the weighted average DRC in the late 1980s was 1.62. This indicates that most industries were competitive at world prices.

While Polish enterprises may, on average, be cost-competitive in most industries, there is almost certainly considerable deviation about the mean. Even in the best enterprises, competitiveness is also strongly influenced by factors unrelated to costs.

From company studies, even potentially good state-owned enterprises tended to demonstrate the following weaknesses (not necessarily in order of importance): weak capital structures and lack of working capital; weak cost and price structure; lack of clear competitive strategies and highly centralised decision-making; technological obsolescence and old equipment in certain production areas; poor quality control in certain areas; weak or non-existent marketing and poor sales capacity; poor product image and lack of product specialisation (although production runs tended to be long and inflexible); a lack of meaningful and timely management information; machine overcapacity, overmanning of indirect labor and staff, and generally low productivity.

On the other hand, the best enterprises demonstrated substantial strengths: a history of profitability and exporting to the West; a well-trained and skilled work force; a loyal work force; lower labour costs than in the West; competent line management and good technical staff; the early recognition by management and workers' councils of the need for change and a commitment to restructure; the ability to improve efficiency by focused commercial management; modern and flexible equipment in certain product areas; a production process that generated only a small amount of waste; brand name recognition in the domestic market and in a few cases, in export markets.

Chapter 4
Policy issues
and recommendations

I.   The present setting

Since 1989, the Polish government's commitment to free markets and private initiative has shaped the framework of industrial restructuring. Under the supervision of the Economic Cabinet, new institutions such as the Ministry of Ownership Changes or the Anti-Monopoly Office have worked to implement the priorities of the Economic Transformation Programme that directly affect industrial restructuring. The main features of the systemic reforms in the areas of privatisation, competition, and price and trade liberalisation have been reviewed in the preceding chapters.

The Ministry of Industry and Trade has found it more difficult to define its role in the new context. For one, it required time-consuming and far-ranging internal reorganisation in order to overcome the inertia of earlier administrative structure. More important, however, is the lack of a clear mandate to prepare an industrial policy strategy. With the notable exception of action through the Industrial Development Agency (see below), it has not been entrusted with tasks that go much beyond its role as a "founding organ" of a large number of state-owned enterprises. In fact, the government has not yet considered a comprehensive industrial policy as a necessary complement to systemic reform.

This does not mean that the government has not acted to promote industrial adjustment by other means. Important initiatives have been taken in four main areas: assistance to enterprises for restructuring, promotion of sectoral restructuring, promotion of exports, and regional development.

Two agencies have been created with specific responsibilities for enterprise restructuring: the Polish Development Bank (PDB) and the Industrial Development Agency (IDA).

The PDB was established by the Council of Ministers in July 1990 to fill a gap in the Polish financial system, which lacked an institution to provide medium and long term (MLT) financing for investment or restructuring. The PDB is essentially an "apex" bank, designed to lend to other banks and only indirectly to enterprises. Due to the underdevelopment of the banking system, however, foreign lenders agreed that the PDB could lend directly to enterprises, on the condition that not more than 15 per cent of its total loans were involved. In addition, only enterprises that have been "commercialised" (converted into a joint stock company and not operating with a workers' council) can borrow from the PDB.

The IDA was founded in January 1991. It succeeded the Industrial Restructuring Fund (IRF) of the Ministry of Industry (now the Ministry of Industry and Trade). The IDA's role is to provide both technical assistance and financing to state-owned enterprises founded by the Ministry of Industry and in need of restructuring.

To date, the food industry is the only sector explicitly targeted by the government and the World Bank as a priority sector. Several technical missions have visited Poland, and considerable funding is planned. The government intends, in particular, to provide investors in the food processing sector with tax concessions.

In another initiative, the government has liberalised imports and has negotiated an industrial export development loan from the World Bank, for a total of $260 million.

Finally, the government has begun to formulate a regional policy. Its goal is to deal with above average unemployment in the coal and steel producing area around Katowice, in the textile producing area around Lodz, in the underdeveloped agricultural areas along Poland's eastern border and elsewhere, and in localities or micro-regions suffering from the "one big firm in a small town" syndrome (cf. OECD, *Regional development problems and policies in Poland*, forthcoming 1992). The government is committed to making better information about regional opportunities more widely available to potential investors and is negotiating with the World Bank for a $300 million loan for regional industrial restructuring.

An interim assessment of these initiatives is difficult and may be premature. But it is worth asking whether some, although useful, can really meet the challenge. The PDB and the IDA in particular have encountered difficulties, as economic developments in Poland since their inception have undermined the measures that they have taken and that their charters allow them to take in the future.

The limitations on the activity of the PDB result in part from a lack of demand for credit, due to the deep recession and general uncertainty. The commercial banking system is at present only providing short-term loans out of its own resources; most banks have shown little interest in providing MLT loans. As a result, the use of available MLT credit from lines funded by external sources such as the World Bank and the European Investment Bank has grown very slowly. Because the PDB is not a development bank that lends at subsidised rates, it has been demanding high, although variable, interest rates. Moreover, its charter only allows the PDB to lend to credit-worthy borrowers. Given the high indebtedness of even many of the best Polish firms, these are hard to find — provided that they were interested in a medium- to long-term loan at high real interest rates in the midst of a deep depression. In Poland today, there is not only a limited supply of credit, there is also a lack of financially sound investment projects.

The IDA has funded the diagnosis of 150 enterprises and the appointment of consultants to undertake detailed restructuring studies in 25 of them. A further 150 diagnostic studies and 100 restructuring studies were scheduled for 1991, although nothing near this number is near completion. The IDA can also use its own resources of around $84 million, inherited from the IRF(Industrial Restructuring Fund), to help state-owned enterprises restructure. However, the government did not allocate any new funds to the IDA in 1991 and has not indicated any plans for additional future funding. The lack of human and financial resources seriously limits the impact that the IDA can have. However, this is not the only problem. With only loose guidelines from the government, the IDA has found it difficult to develop and use clear criteria for selecting enterprises to assist and establishing its loan policy. It has taken on financial commitments to a number of enterprises, in some cases large one, and the likelihood that the loans will be repaid appears low. As of January 1992, IDA had trouble meeting even its current commitments.

With respect to the industrial export development loan from the World Bank, total commitments in 1991 exceeded $100 million, but most of the funds were designated for financing the imports necessary for exports. Poland does not yet have an incentive system for expanding exports.

Whatever the merits of the measures implemented to facilitate the industrial restructuring process, they fail to meet the challenge of a situation which has deteriorated, so that the premises on which measures have been founded are no longer valid. Specifically, privatisation has proved a far more lengthy process than originally anticipated, the law on bankruptcy has been difficult to implement, and a liberalised and efficient capital market is emerging only slowly. Moreover, the persistence of inflation, rising unemployment, and falling output are more problematic than originally predicted. Under these circumstances, the measure taken to date to assist restructuring are both insufficient in themselves and insufficiently related to other objectives, including privatisation and stabilisation. For practical reasons, more active promotion of restructuring will be a necessary condition for extensive privatisation and widespread industrial recovery.

II. Policy options for the future

A. Choosing the general approach

A minimalist approach to the industrial restructuring problems that arise at the present stage of the transition to a full-fledged market economy would entail:

— Continued reduction of the role of government in the economy and strengthening of institutions to improve the legal basis of privatisation and reduction of monopoly power. This would mean in particular strengthening the banking system and perfecting the framework for mass privatisation (e.g. the creation of national investment funds), for privatisation through individual sales (e.g. developing the so-called "sectoral approach"), and for privatisation through liquidation (e.g. clarifying the legal status of property).

— Improving and/or accelerating the implementation of the complementary measures already in place. For example, the IDA's risk management performance could be improved by better definition of its banking criteria or better co-ordination with the Ministry of Ownership Changes. The process of formulating a regional policy could also be speeded up, as could the implementation of the programme to promote the food processing industry.

1. The limits of a minimalist approach

This minimalist approach would have merits. It involves very little risk of aggravating market distortions and requires the fewest resources. In the short run, it avoids two socio-economic pitfalls: first, the opposition from trade unions and workers' councils to any policy that would give "privileges" to some enterprises while allowing others to lay off personnel and go bankrupt; second, the weakness of public civil service, which lacks the experience, resources, and efficient organisation necessary to design and manage "sophisticated" microeconomic policies in a market context.

Nevertheless, it has shortcomings:

First, even if it were the best way to maximise net long-term benefits, it might entail a politically unsustainable distribution of structural adjustment costs and benefits. Given the extent of market imperfections due to the immature financial and labour markets, an exclusively market-determined adjustment would likely carry high costs in terms of unemployment and lost output in the short to medium term. Such costs might well exceed what is socially acceptable: the current unemployment level is probably close to the maximum that Poland's social safety net can handle in the present budgetary context, and budget constraints are not likely to ease in the near future.

Second, the approach may even not be the best in the long term. Market failures may not only slow the adjustment process and defer some of its benefits. They may also cause the adjustment process to deviate from the optimal path and thus reduce the long-term potential for growth. Without support from a far-sighted and experienced financial system, a number of potentially viable enterprises might fail to adapt and be forced to close down. If the process of "creative destruction" that characterises transition is excessively biased towards destruction, the potential for growth will diminish. It would be difficult to offset this loss in the future, given the outlook for savings and the limited capability for retraining human capital.

Third, improvement of the measures that currently complement systemic reforms may not suffice to address the challenge. Selective, stand-alone programmes designed to deal with special problems often do not work well in isolation and, if they are not co-ordinated, may work at cross purposes. But there is a more fundamental reason. As long as there is no broad, decisive action to change a situation in which most state-owned enterprises have neither the means nor the incentives to restructure, the efficiency of these measures will remain limited.

As a result, if the government adheres to the minimalist approach, it may face a dilemma:

— It is difficult to strengthen incentives, which means above all imposing hard budget constraints through the threat of bankruptcy, because of social resistance in the concerned enterprises and because of the risk of a chain reaction leading to closures of viable as well as non-viable firms; but

— if the government accepts a relative softness of budget restraints, as a substitute for measures to compensate for market failures, and if it hesitates to put non-viable enterprises into bankruptcy on a scale sufficient to signal a new policy, this can only enlarge the structural adjustment gap, with cascading negative effects on the privatisation process, the financial system, the State budget, and, more generally, macroeconomic performance.

2. A role for an industrial policy

If the minimalist approach were complemented by an active industrial and trade policy, the government could, under certain conditions, escape the dilemma.

The basic rationale

By taking this approach, Poland would in fact follow the example of OECD countries. Most of them have had to supplement market forces with transitory measures designed to accelerate industrial adjustment to sudden and major changes in the economic environment, such as the two oil crises. In addition, some countries (e.g. Ireland, Portugal and Spain) have implemented broad-ranging policies to help their industry face challenges and exploit opportunities arising from their integration into regional and world markets. Of course, the experience of OECD countries does not offer any ready-made model to fit Poland's particular needs. But there are certain basic lessons that have been collectively drawn by OECD countries[11] and that underlie the recently issued EC guidelines on industrial policy[12]. These lessons are, to a large extent, relevant to Poland.

In a market context, industrial policy can contribute to economic development in three ways:

— It can *compensate for market failures*. Market imperfections are widespread, but do not all require corrective action by the government. State intervention can be legitimate when major market failures can block or distort industrial adjustment. Specific incentives can stimulate deficient market forces or amplify weak market signals. In Poland, they could conceivably accelerate the reform of the best companies caught in a short run crunch, and expedite the establishment of the corporate governance structures necessary for a broad-based industrial recovery in the long run.

— It can *provide catalysts for industrial development*. Market mechanisms cannot work properly without them but cannot produce them. They consist of material and intangible infrastructures and include, in particular, transport and telecommunication infrastructures, training facilities, technical and product quality standards, and a public procurement framework. In Poland, budget constraints and the absolute priority given to some areas, such as privatisation, should not result in minimising the importance given to such catalysts.

— It can *accelerate industrial adjustment.* Two elements play a crucial role in determining the adaptability of economic structures: 1) the technology diffusion network; and 2) small and medium-sized enterprises, especially in manufacturing or professional services activities. In Poland, the disintegration of in-house research and development must be halted; the old technological infrastructure should be recast and a large-scale modern technology diffusion network should be implemented immediately; specific obstacles that stand in the way of creating or developing *industrial* SMEs should receive more attention in the overall policy of promoting the private sector.

More active industrial restructuring to attain macroeconomic objectives

Under the special conditions of transition towards a market economy, there is another justification for an industrial policy. During this phase, macroeconomic/microeconomic interaction is not working as it does in mature market economies. Macroeconomic policies can have perverse effects on microeconomic structures and behaviour if the obstacles to restructuring are too high. And delays in industrial restructuring may make macroeconomic objectives more and more difficult to achieve.

Industrial policy can help shortening these delays. The approach is to amplify market incentives for enterprises with the greatest competitive potential — and sanctions for non performing ones — in the framework of aggregate credit constraints which could be eased as inflationary pressures recede as a result of increased efficiency in the industrial sector.

B. Promoting industrial restructuring

Certain prerequisites are necessary if industrial policy is to perform its task efficiently, especially when financial support is involved. Some are general in nature and apply in any market economy, whether mature or in transition. Others are specific to the Polish situation.

1. Prerequisites

Among the general prerequisites, securing *a stable macroeconomic environment* for industry is paramount. Although industrial policy can help achieve macroeconomic objectives, it cannot be a substitute for a sound macroeconomic policy. And the best contribution that macroeconomic policy can make to industrial adjustment is to prevent inflation and other disequilibria from encouraging short-sighted and speculative behaviour and discouraging long-term domestic and foreign investment. As the recent *OECD Economic Survey*[1] pointed out, an expansionary macroeconomic policy is not, at this stage, a realistic option for accelerating economic recovery. A second prerequisite relates to the *tax system*, which should be seen by investors as transparent, fair and stable. Delays in completing tax reform are understandable, given the inherent difficulties, but are nevertheless unfortunate. Finally, the experience of OECD countries shows that *competition* is a key to effective industrial change. In Poland, despite the rapid improvement of domestic competitive structures, foreign competitive pressures will continue to play a vital role. It is therefore important that a liberal import policy be maintained, but it is equally important that Polish firms not be artificially deprived of greater exposure to the stimuli of international competition in export markets.

In a strategy worked out in 1990 and still in force, the development of the private sector was to be the primary means of restructuring the industrial sector, through privatisation and the creation of new firms; it was recognised that, before they could enter the privatisation process, many state-owned enterprises would have to be transformed. Only limited efforts were made to begin the restructuring process. The government lacks resources due to its precarious budgetary situation, but it also lacks confidence in the ability of state-owned enterprises to use investment resources efficiently.

If the latter are to obtain public support, in the form of new credits or of financial restructuring to alleviate debt burdens, the disincentives to maximise their market value through sound restructuring prior to privatisation must be removed. As indicated above, strengthening and perfecting the bankruptcy process is a fundamental objective in this respect. The recent *OECD Economic Survey*[1] offers suggestions on how to achieve this goal. However, this may take some time, especially in view of the institutional requirements.

When deciding on measures to support the restructuring of state-owned enterprises before incentive structures have been completely fixed, the government must weigh the *urgency* of the issue. It may judge too high the risk that potentially viable enterprises will fail before they are relieved of the nuisance created by non-viable (and non-liquidated) firms or financially restructured through a better bankruptcy process. In that case, it may consider including in its short-term policy agenda more active measures to support industrial restructuring.

2. Policy objectives and priorities

A time schedule should be established for attaining the objectives of an industrial restructuring policy. Some are urgent and should be implemented immediately; others are medium-term goals. This does not mean taking a sequential approach. All relevant actions should be initiated as soon as possible, including those which require a longer implementation period and can bring significant results only in the medium to long run.

In the most urgent category, the process of industrial restructuring must be unblocked by reducing the obstacles that prevent market mechanisms from: a) selecting potentially viable firms; and b) providing reliable signals for reallocating resources that are devoted to non-viable activities and therefore obstruct the privatisation process. The most significant obstacles are: firm indebtedness (to the government, the banking system, or other firms); the corporate governance of state-owned enterprises; and the structural deficiencies of the capital market, which lead to conservative risk management that is detrimental to the efficient use of very scarce financial resources.

The primary short-term objective would be to implement temporary measures to facilitate the necessary reallocation of industrial assets and liabilities by the nascent financial system. This process involves selecting enterprises and investment projects. Such selection is a routine task in an efficient capital market in mature market economies; but in the transitional phase in Poland, it has to be stimulated by non-market institutions to some extent. For reasons given in previous chapters, the selection must be made according to criteria that extend beyond immediate enterprise profitability and financial solvency. Other short-term objectives include: financing training programmes designed to increase firms' management capabilities; and reducing the social burdens of restructuring.

For medium-term objectives, more attention must be given to promoting the development of private SMEs in the productive sector; to redressing the most acute micro-regional and sectoral imbalances; and to exploiting the opportunities for enabling specific industries to act as growth poles. Demand-side policies, particularly with respect to government procurement, need to be elaborated as a way of ensuring consistency between government purchase practices and the overall industrial restructuring strategy.

3. Two basic principles: selectivity and conditionality

In mature market economies, policies to promote industrial competitiveness and development have become more and more horizontal in character; they do not generally discriminate between enterprises and sectors. In Poland, the efficiency of horizontal measures *alone* would be limited as long as the market selection process remains too weak to purge the industrial structure of non-viable firms.

Selectivity at the firm level

Under these conditions, the principle of selectivity warrants adoption. In Poland, selectivity should operate at the level of the firm rather than the industry. Policy should be oriented to promoting the restructuring of viable firms regardless of industry, rather than promoting "promising" industries. At this stage, the pattern of Polish sectoral competitive advantage is unclear. Industry level studies undertaken with a view towards promoting privatisation have tended to conclude that it is impossible to generalise about the way to proceed on the basis of industrial sectors. Apart from, say, food processing, it is not known which industries are likely to succeed in the long run, and viable firms should not be penalised simply because they belong to alleged "unpromising" industries[13]. The increasing number of firm-level studies undertaken by foreign and Polish consultants to aid privatisation should facilitate the identification of firms that may be expected to be competitive after restructuring.

Selectivity at the firm level is also in keeping with the overall approach of the Ministry of Ownership Changes, which has opted not for one method of privatisation but for many, tailored to the situation of particular enterprises. However, it is appropriate to take a more industry-oriented approach in two exceptional cases: first, the evidently promising industries, of which food processing is the best example; and second, the hard-hit heavy industries of particular regions. For the latter, with a history of over-investment and structural distortions, it is worth trying to help firms identify their residual underlying comparative advantages in order to give broad direction to capacity cutting and reinvestment, for example, in smaller, modern facilities.

A central objective must be to create, through appropriate incentives, means to weed out the bad enterprises and enable the promising ones to improve management practices, restructure, and consequently increase the credibility of the bankruptcy threat for the others. The incentive system should aim to open restructuring opportunities. To be efficient it should ensure that potential beneficiaries (banks or enterprises) bear the risks associated with their decision on how to seize these opportunities.

Conditional support

Conditionality is also a key to escaping the past system of subsidisation. Conditionality means that financial assistance for restructuring should only be granted in exchange for the attainment of specific standards of performance that should be easy to monitor. Instead of adopting a centralised approach, government should stimulate firms to propose initiatives. Firms should be made responsible, through a competitive process, for demonstrating that they can achieve medium-term profitability in exchange for public assistance to restructure. The public bodies concerned would either accept, reject or modify the firms' proposals; they would not dictate them.

4. Choosing the policy instruments

The choice of instruments to be used in implementing industrial restructuring policy must take into account four main requirements:

— first, at a time of great financial stringency, excessive public spending must be avoided;
— second, the creation of new institutions that would aggravate the problem of co-ordinating policy must be minimised;
— third, the scarcity of human resources and the desirability of creating a critical mass must be recognised; and
— fourth, the use of foreign technical assistance must be optimised.

The instruments should also enhance co-ordination between the promotion of privatisation through industrial restructuring, on the one hand, and, on the other, the pursuit of other industrial, macroeconomic, and social policies — in particular, in the areas of trade, foreign investment, competition, training, regional development, public procurement, and science and technology.

III. Recommendations

A. Urgent action

To allow privatisation to proceed and to minimise further declines in output and employment, the most urgent task is to reinforce the processes by which potentially viable firms can be distinguished from less promising ones. Among the latter, it is worth drawing a distinction between the "dinosaurs" — ultra-large employers with chronic over-investment and weak customer bases — and the others, many of which are relatively small in scale. The "dinosaurs" may require special treatment because of their regional character and their large social impact.

Another urgent task is to determine the structure of enterprise debt and then arrange solutions that are consistent with protecting viable firms against the non-viable ones. Finally, a politically realistic plan of action for unpromising enterprises needs to be spelled out.

The options available for carrying out each of these tasks will now be discussed. In general, these are temporary emergency measures rather than mechanisms that would become permanent features of Poland's industrial landscape.

1. Accelerating the market selection process

There are two interrelated elements of the restructuring process. The first is the need to devise a procedure to identify and select the firms to restructure actively in a population of some 7 000 state industrial enterprises. Selectivity is necessary, as it is widely agreed that not all these enterprises hold future promise and that unpromising enterprises act as a drain in the competition for scarce financial and human resources. The second is the need to specify precisely the incentives to be made available to the most promising enterprises. Appropriate incentives fall into two categories: incentives that "clean up" indebtedness (debt restructuring) and incentives that help firms invest on the basis of potential profitability.

The policy options theoretically available can be ranked according to the degree of direct government involvement in the selection process. There are obvious reasons for giving the lowest priority to solutions involving administrative allocation of resources. But other considerations such as timing must be taken into account, and this complicates the choice.

Helping firms to restructure their debt is probably a condition for reindustrialising, so debt restructuring is of paramount short-run importance. Once the enterprise indebtedness problem has been tackled, efforts can be made to strengthen the competitive assets of most promising enterprises.

(i) Restructuring enterprise debt

To be efficient, any solution to the debt problem presupposes a parallel effort to strengthen financial discipline in the enterprise sector. Improvement of "flow" conditions must accompany actions to deal with "stock" problems of unsustainable financial structure.

Enterprise debt is of three types: debt to the banking system for principal/interest owed, debt to the government (for back taxes, social security, etc.), and inter-firm debt. Whatever the approach taken, debt restructuring should be based on an indebtedness inventory conducted by the Ministry of Ownership Changes (MOC) and the Ministry of Industry and Trade (MIT) in co-operation with the Ministry of Finance. Tracing enterprise liabilities is fairly straightforward, because information can be provided by the tax administration and the banking system. In addition, at the start of restructuring, the government might give all firms a short deadline, say one month, to post their outstanding debt claims against other firms. This would give the MOC/MIT a fairly complete mapping of firm indebtedness.

Three approaches to handling the issue of bank debt restructuring in a manner consistent with the government's industrial restructuring strategy can be considered. Each has merits and drawbacks. The details of these approaches are not spelled out there, but the technicalities may be important in practice. In the first, all firms receive debt relief. In the second, the government chooses the most promising enterprises for restructuring and, therefore, for debt relief. In the third, which appears to be the most efficient, a mixed approach allows the institutions that hold enterprise debt to select which firms' debt to restructure (see Insert 1).

(ii) Assisting promising enterprises to restructure

(a) Government debt relief

In addition to relieving promising firms of their bank debt, the government might consider relieving them of their debt to the budget (for back taxes and social security payments). Thus far, firms have resisted restructuring in part because it has been perceived as holding very few benefits. Now, to win their co-operation, the government could introduce carrots in addition to sticks. It would have to specify an envelope of benefits to be made available to promising enterprises that restructure, but it must also keep in mind the need to contain public expenditures in the interests of preventing inflation and the crowding out of savings. The Ministry of Finance would have to decide upon the ultimate size of the restructuring

INSERT 1

Three ways to select enterprises for bank debt relief

1. Debt relief for all firms

The indebtedness to banks of all firms would be totally or partly canceled, regardless of the firm's promise as a viable entity. This approach would strengthen the banking system, and a strong banking system is of critical importance to the development of a market economy. By forgiving all the bad debts of firms, the banking system would be relieved of the burden of non-performing loans. With a clean slate, it could begin to act more aggressively to attract savings and, taking the associated risks, make loans for reindustrialisation.

The disadvantages of this approach, however, are many. First, it is very costly to the government; it would increase the budget deficit and fuel inflation, since the Treasury would have to assume the totality of the banking system's bad loans. Second, it would have a negative impact on the motivation and morale of the enterprises that tried to pay their debts as well as on the private sector. Third, it fails to provide any information about creditors' judgement of the viability of enterprises, information that would help the government define its liquidation or support policy. Fourth, if only part of the debt was canceled, firms would undoubtedly pressure government to relieve still more. The process would tend to be endless.

2. Government selection of promising enterprises

The Ministry of Ownership Change (MOC) and the Ministry of Industry and Trade (MIT) would draw up together a list of promising enterprises. This would be feasible because each ministry, and the MOC in particular, has been collecting data, conducting its own enterprise studies, and directing complementary studies by consultants in order to identify companies with market potential. The criteria for a promising enterprise with market potential would be made as clear and transparent as possible. They should not be restricted to immediate profitability and solvency. Instead, a composite measure of potential performance should be developed, including variables such as a firm's past history of profitability and exporting to the West, its production and operation management, product design, human resource capability, and so forth.

The process of identifying promising firms is certain to be imperfect. It would entail a political burden and would subject the government to lobbying. Moreover, it might well omit some promising enterprises and include some unpromising ones. In the case of the former German Democratic Republic, for example, the Truehand now estimates that some one-third of all state-owned enterprises are not worth restructuring. Assuming that the industrial performance of Poland and the GDR were about similar, this suggests that only about 2 300 Polish enterprises, rather than 6 000, are altogether

(see following page)

unworthy of restructuring. In addition, the state-owned enterprises left out of the list of promising firms would have to have the opportunity to appeal their status. The process and the ensuing investigation would probably be cumbersome. At that stage, determined action by pressure groups could even block the whole process.

3. The banking system selects its most promising clients for debt relief

Banks would be given an incentive to participate actively in the selection of potentially viable enterprises. A trade-off would allow banks to benefit from relief of part of the debt owed by firms. A mechanism should therefore ensure that banks pick enterprises with the greatest competitive promise rather than those with the most short-term indebtedness. Such a mechanism could involve debt-for-equity swaps or other formulae, depending on the government's views concerning the long-term development of bank/industry relationships.

While this mixed solution would also imply budgetary costs, its advantages are considerable. A principle of holding prominent actors in the nascent capital market financially responsible for their decisions would be initiated. A process of identifying promising and unpromising firms would also be started, and their creditors would be involved. There would be less opportunity for political lobbying than under the second option, and the banking system would be strengthened as in the first option.

envelope, but some debt relief would pave the way for increased co-operation.

The government could use the restructuring of this debt as an occasion to: a) improve the management of these firms; and b) set up machinery that could conceivably provide the foundation for further mass privatisation or other forms of privatisation that the MOC has successfully tried. Insert 2 sets out an illustrative scenario for implementing this approach.

(b) Loan guarantees

Debt relief will make access to working capital far easier. As mentioned above, Poland's new banks are increasingly making short-term loans. Once state-owned enterprises have become more credit-worthy due to debt relief, they should be able to obtain loans for working capital more easily. Nevertheless, the cost of working capital will probably be higher in Poland than in competitor countries for the foreseeable future.

It is unrealistic to imagine that enough investment capital from overseas can be made available to restructure at a price approximating world prices and processed quickly enough, i.e. within the next two years, to finance the needs of all promising enterprises[14]. This is probably so even assuming an average cost per enterprise of only $ 1.5 million (the cost proposed in Chapter 3) and excluding the needs of the "dinosaurs". It will thus be necessary to establish rules for allocating scarce resources.

As noted in Chapter 3, a number of credit lines are being opened and guaranteed by foreign governments, but only a small proportion of the

---

INSERT 2

Illustrative scenario for improving the management of promising state-owned enterprises in view of their privatisation

The debt owed to the government in the form of back taxes could be converted into "shares" vested in temporary, newly created financial intermediaries. These would initially be semi-public joint stock companies, acting independently of the government on a day-to-day basis. Ultimately, these shares could be distributed as "vouchers" to citizens, and the newly created financial intermediaries could be converted into privately managed mutual funds, as the MOC envisaged in its mass privatisation plan. In the first six months, however, these shares would have no financial value, since distributing them to the public as saleable vouchers could be highly inflationary. They would merely be an accounting representation of the past tax obligations of promising enterprises, which, in effect, would be written off.

The semi-public institutional investors themselves would be responsible for selecting the firms for government debt relief. This would provide yet another means — shielded from the full force of political influence — to identify promising enterprises.

In practical terms, the establishment of financial intermediaries managed by Polish professionals (perhaps assisted by foreign experts) would have as its chief virtue the opportunity to improve the management of promising enterprises. A total of, say, six financial intermediaries could hold voting shares in 1 000 firms. Each officer of a financial intermediary could have, say, 10 firms under his jurisdiction. This would require the employment of a total of 100 officers. Voting rights acquired through this debt-for-"equity" swap should be vigorously exercised by the financial intermediaries for two purposes: to break deadlocks between managers and workers' council representatives and to help promising state-owned-enterprises restructure. State-owned enterprises need immediate guidance to foreign banking procedures in order to tap fresh sources of investment finance.

This proposal to improve management could be implemented through the Ministry of Ownership Changes. It could be financed with loans designated for privatisation, inasmuch as the creation of financial intermediaries can be viewed as a first step in its implementation. The experience of the 100 officers hired to help improve the management of promising state-owned enterprises might also be considered an investment to train Polish professionals for participation in mass privatisation.

funds theoretically available has been used. The Ministry of Finance estimates that, as of July 1991, the sum total of credits contracted by Polish enterprises and guaranteed by a foreign government amounted to only $220 million. These delays are partly attributed to lack of experience with foreign banking procedures, the reluctance of Polish banks to distribute credits, and the fact that only one Polish bank (Bank Handlowy) has been registered in the West.

One purpose of installing management specialists in promising Polish state-owned enterprises (see Insert 2) would be to help expedite the flow of foreign capital to these end-users. However, this will not help Polish banks enter the process of on-lending. To induce them to do so and to provide promising state-owned enterprises with immediate investment capital for restructuring at a reasonable interest rate, the government must offer more support.

As one possibility, the Polish government could provide guarantees to Polish banks for on-lending to promising enterprises. Insert 3 sets out a scenario for such a support programme.

INSERT 3

Illustrative scenario for supporting promising enterprises through credit guarantees

The MOC has selected roughly 400 state-owned enterprises for priority privatising due to their promise as competitive enterprises. A first objective might be to guarantee an average loan of $1.5 million to about one-third of them over a two year period (at a cost of approximately $495 million plus some $5 million for overhead) in the form of a credit guarantee for restructuring.

The firms should be selected through a process of competition among qualified state-owned enterprises, those chosen for debt relief (see Insert 1). Every applicant for a guaranteed loan would be required to prepare, with the assistance of its management assistant representative from a financial intermediary (see Insert 2), a short two year business plan. The plan would specify how the state-owned enterprise intended to restructure. The applicant would propose performance standards to be attained in two years, including output, quality, and export targets. The government credit garantee would be allocated on this basis, and the applicants would commit themselves to these performance targets in exchange for government support.

The administration could be handled by the Industrial Development Agency of the Ministry of Industry and Trade.

(iii) The treatment of unpromising enterprises

These firms present a major problem for the Ministry of Ownership Changes because their prospects for privatisation are grim. There is little likelihood that buyers will be found in the foreseeable future, and political considerations have slowed "privatising" their assets, or part of them, through liquidation.

As noted earlier, it is thought that a large number of Poland's industrial state-owned enterprises (roughly 5 000) account for only some 20 per cent of total industrial employment. Presumably, a significant proportion are non-viable firms. Nevertheless, wholesale closures are probably not politically realistic at the present time. Therefore, political and economic objectives must be balanced when recommending a policy different from the present one, which, for all practical purposes, is doing little about non-viable state-owned enterprises.

Two advantages to the government of the present course are that open unemployment is not being increased and that they may be collecting taxes, if the state-owned enterprises in question are still paying them. But there are also two disadvantages. In a market economy, non-viable enterprises are a burden because they use scarce resources inefficiently. In Poland today, however, many resources are no longer scarce because of the economic depression. Nevertheless, non-viable enterprises remain a burden because many are part of the inter-firm debt market and harm viable enterprises by adding to their debt burden. Moreover, virtually all non-viable enterprises now appear to be beyond the control of their owners ("founding" ministries). They operate as best they can, more or less autonomously. In some companies, self-management has led to abuses, including theft.

The government has operated on the principle that privatisation should not be free: if a firm is sold, or if ownership is transferred from the government to a private party, the new owner must pay a price for the enterprise. The principle is sensible, but it is competing with another equally sensible principle that has become more compelling since 1989. It is that control of an enterprise entails the obligation of ownership.

Instead of maintaining a do-nothing policy towards non-viable state-owned enterprises, the government could: a) make more intense use of the bankruptcy procedure; and b) when this is not appropriate, sell the enterprise for a nominal sum to the managers and workers who control it, thereby joining ownership and control.

2. Export incentives

Export activity constitutes a highly promising avenue to recovery of output and employment levels in Poland. Consequently, the government and its major international financial supporters have taken a strong stand in favour of an export-led development strategy. Yet they have adopted few concrete measures to stimulate exports per se. Trade policy, including export policy, has largely focused on liberalising imports, on the notion that it is necessary to import easily in order to increase exports of acceptable international standards of quality. Moreover, the lion's share of loans earmarked for exports has gone for imports.

The new Polish Export Development Bank (EDB) has two World Bank credit lines, one for agro-industry and one for industrial exports. Its loans tend to be small, on the order of $50 000, and interest rates are market-determined (except for loans made available by the French government, which have subsidised interest rates). Even though Poland's capital market is theoretically completely open, interest rates for loans in zlotys are determined by the market forces operating in Poland, while those of loans in dollars are determined by "international" market forces. Most of the EDB's customers for foreign credit are international trucking companies. According to the EDB, the foreign exchange law only permits lending in foreign currency (at an interest rate of approximately 9 per cent) for purposes of importing 15.

In theory, Polish companies can borrow in international capital markets to finance their exports. In practice, they don't know how to do so, they probably cannot do so, and government controls over foreign exchange are such that they may not do so. As a result, trade policy in Poland supports imports rather than exports.

Export activity in virtually all OECD countries receives more direct and indirect government support than in Poland. It is sometimes supported by an export-import bank which lends at favorable terms, but Poland lacks such a bank. It is also almost always supported by government-maintained networks abroad, a practice largely unknown in Poland.

In the late-industrialising countries that will offer Poland competition in many foreign markets, exports are frequently given preferential credit, exemption from import duties on inputs, and possibly tax holidays.

To level the playing field, the Polish government might introduce an incentive system open to any firm that can produce a letter of credit as proof of export activity, whether that firm is public or private, "promising" or "unpromising". It should be possible to raise the capital for these export loans, if not from the big international lenders, then from the individual governments that have already promised Poland lines of credit.

B. Industrial policy in the medium term

The importance of easing the privatisation "traffic jam" and of relieving some of most severe current economic problems — such as firm insolvency — should not obscure the need to prepare medium-term industrial policies. These should address five areas: technological capability and small and medium-sized enterprises; regional development; the environment; sectoral restructuring and foreign investment; and procurement.

1. Technological capability and small and medium-sized enterprises

The basic legal conditions for private entrepreneurship, such as property rights and company law, now exist, but remaining administrative and legal obstacles to SME creation and development must be removed. These obstacles include the fear of reprivatisation (or restitution of ownership to previous owners), restrictions on the use of real estate that encumber mortgage lending, and excessively bureaucratic company registration procedures.

Even if these administrative and legal obstacles are removed, there remain firm grounds for arguing for further support to SMEs[16], because of the many "market failures" in the supply of technology, finance, and commercial services to SMEs, and because of the limited access of SMEs to export markets and government procurement contracts. In the area of finance, for example, lending institutions are often reluctant to incur the administrative costs of small loans and are frequently unwilling to risk uncollateralised loans altogether. Lacking capital, SMEs are in a poor position to develop their technological and managerial bases. Finance is sure to be an acute problem, given the underdevelopment of Poland's capital market and the virtual nonexistence of venture-capital institutions.

In addition, the social returns to helping SMEs are frequently high, because of their positive spillovers and externalities. In the manufacturing sector, a dynamic SME population typically means efficient supplies of parts and components. This helps the whole manufacturing sector achieve low-cost, high-quality, and on-time production. In the service sector, SMEs often provide an efficient distribution network, which also keeps costs down and service quality up.

In the most developed countries, increasing attention is given by governments to the adjustment challenges facing SMEs in the emerging

INSERT 4

Support to SME development
in Portugal and the German eastern Länder

Portugal's PEDIP programme is a comprehensive set of infrastructural and institutional modernisation measures for industry, coupled with financial support to overcome market failures, improve innovation and technological upgrading, and increase investment. Particular attention is given to SMEs.

The major part of total PEDIP funding comes from the European Community. About two-thirds of the direct transfers come from the EC and the remaining one-third from the Portuguese government. Including loans for private sector moderni-sation and improvement from the European Investment Bank of ECU 1 billion, the total of transfers and loan funding is ECU 2.5 billion ($3.1 billion at $1.25/ECU). Gross EC transfers for reform and modernisation have been large: in 1989, they were as much as 2.5 per cent of Portugal's GDP (cf. OECD, Economic Survey of Portugal, 1989).

Technological innovation, an essential component of competitiveness and a key factor in the development of Portuguese industry, is a main focal area of PEDIP. Various programmes are designed to improve technological capability through: 1) rationalisation of distribution and transport; 2) development of technological capacity in enterprises and universities, and linkages between the two actors; 3) development of human resources; 4) investment in modernisation of productive capacity; 5) creation of a risk guarantee system for SMES; 6) improvement of pro-ductivity and quality at the enterprise, industry, and national levels; and 7) diffusion of best-practice techniques throughout Portuguese industry.

To raise living standards in the new Länder and Berlin (East), the German government has adopted measures to aid businesses, including SMEs. There are SME programs to promote: business consultancy; information and training events for entrepreneurs, managers, skilled workers and persons setting up in business; facilities outside companies for vocational training and technology transfer; and innovation (including R&D for SMEs and industry-related support measures of the Federal Ministry for Research and Technology).

For SMEs, investment incentives and various tax credits can amount to as much as 47 per cent of the investment (see "Economic Assistance in the New German Länder", Federal Ministry of Economics, 1991).

Table 18. Features of selected consultancy, advisory and technology diffusion programmes in OECD countries

	Australia NIES	Canada AMTAP	Denmark CIM	Germany FUKMU	France LOGIC	Ireland Technology Audit	Japan Kohsetsushi	Norway BUNT	Portugal PEDIP	United Kingdom Consultancy Initiatives	United States NYS[1] ITES/IEP
Service areas supported											
Technology assistance	x	x	x	x	x	x	x	x	x	x	x
Training human resources	x	x			x	x	x	x			x
Business planning	x	x	x	x	x	x	x	x	x	x	x
Design	x					x		x	x	x	
Quality	x	x		x		x	x	x	x	x	x
Marketing	x				x	x		x	x	x	x
Financial/Management systems	x	x	x	x	x	x	x	x	x	x	x
Assisted firm size	SMEs	20-100 employees	SMEs	Industry <DM 10 M turnover (general consultancy)	<500 employees	<Ir£3 M turnover <60 employees <300 employees	<¥100 M capital <300 employees	<300 employees	Mainly SMEs	<500 employees	<500 employees
Length of support	Variable	Variable implementation in some cases	Variable		Variable implementation in some cases	10-15 days	Usually short	15-20 days	Variable	15 days	Variable
Cost-sharing (public sector share)	50%	Maximum 75%	75-25%	50-60%	50%	75-50%	100-50%	75%	50%	50% (66% in special areas)	50% maximum
Number of firms supported per year	1 800	200	140	9 000		120	25 000	100	200 guidance	15 000	150 multi-firm projects

1. The New York State programmes are given as an example. There are numerous US state-level initiatives and they vary greatly.

Source : OECD adapted from national studies.

global economy[17]. Extensive support to SMEs is widespread in OECD countries, especially in the areas of: 1) assistance in gaining access to financing; 2) improvement in the provision of training, information, counselling, and technical aid; and 3) enhancement of export potential, an increasingly important policy measure as the production system becomes more global. Features of selected consultancy, advisory, and technology diffusion programmes are shown in Table 18. Portugal and unified Germany offer two models of support to SMEs in a catching-up process (see Insert 4).

2. Regional development   (see Maps in the Annex)

The OECD Industry Committee has recently reviewed Poland's regional problems. Its report[18] concludes that regional policy in Poland should have two main objectives: a) to facilitate the overall structural adjustment now in progress; and b) to cushion its most dramatic impacts.

For the first objective, the Committee underlines the need to avoid concentrating support on problem regions to the detriment of the most dynamic parts of the country:

> It would probably be dangerous to ignore the areas with the greatest economic potential: Warsaw, Poznan, Gdansk-Gdynia, Bydgoszcz-Torun, Wroclaw. They have an industrial tradition, they have universities and research centers, they have a better-than-the-others accessibility to Western Europe, they have a diversified industrial base, they have a qualified labour force, they probably have more capital and entrepreneurship, they are more likely to attract foreign capital. They, more than the rest of the country, can be the locomotives that will draw the Polish economy. If structural megadjustment is to succeed, it is in these areas. It is therefore reasonable to suggest that they should receive some priority in governmental action, particularly in terms of infrastructure.

> The strengthening of these areas might imply some increase in inter-regional disparities. This risk is probably worth taking. Such disparities are at present rather small, and a slight increase would not be surprising nor unbearable. In all countries, economic growth has, in its initial stages, been accompanied by an increase in inter-regional differences. In a second stage, these disparities tend to diminish. But Poland has not yet reached this second stage.

For the second objective, the report distinguishes between two situations: the regions of old industrialisation such as Upper Silesia and the less developed rural eastern regions (such as Zamosz). For the former it advocates:

> *Central government initiatives to plan and assist decline of the tradi-tional industries, especially mining and steel industry, as well as local initiatives to exploit in new, more promising activities, the develop-ment potential, especially the existing stock of human capital.*

For the latter, the report stresses the role of agriculture and related activities in overall economic development:

> *On the whole, agriculture has a key role to play in regional policy, as a shock absorber, as a basis for the development of food industry, and as an important productive sector. It should not fall victim of unfair competition (trade barriers or subsidised imports).*

Poland also has a problem that raises the question of the relationship between regional and industrial policy. A number of "micro-regions" have been hit very hard by recession. They often have severe ecological problems and depend on a single large firm, typically in heavy industry. One case is the large firm in a small town, as in Praszka, Brzeszcze, Leszczyny, and Kleczew. A greater social problem is caused in larger towns dominated by a firm responsible for the livelihood of the town itself, as in Starachowice, Stalowa, Wola and Mielec. Many of these regions are unli-kely to restructure "spontaneously", given their low level of diversification and their lack of attractiveness to foreign investors.

An active industrial policy aimed at selectively revitalising such regions is needed, possibly on the model of Spain's regional programme (see Insert 5). Regional development (or reconversion) corporations might be formed with seed capital provided by the central government, local authorities, private investors, foreign governments, and international organisations and firms. These corporations could help create and then assist new SMEs and networks of enterprises (sub-contractors) to under-take public initiatives, such as public works infrastructure, environmental clean-up, and other projects that contribute to the resumption of regional growth.

3. Environmental aspects of industrial policy

In the past Poland made substantial investments in heavy industry, often deliberately located in highly populated areas. Anti-pollution safe-guards were frequently inadequate. The high level of subsidies, and the low price of coal, led to an inefficient and high polluting usage of coal resources. In Poland, coal accounts for 79 per cent of primary energy

INSERT 5

Regional policy in Spain
The ZUR Programme

The objectives of ZUR — the regional measures adopted in Spain to set up "Urgent Reindustrialisation Zones" — went beyond the mere promotion of investments or job-generating projects. One of its main aims was to rebuild the industrial structure of hard-hit regions. It used a global standard for optimum diversification and granted benefits to submitted projects on the basis of their contribution to the endogenous development of an area.

The projects and investments located in municipal districts included in the ZUR areas could obtain subsidies, preferential access to official credits, fiscal benefits, and easy access to industrial sites and technical and management assistance. Subsidies could reach 30 per cent of the approved investment, and be used for fixed assets, R&D, engineering expenditure and other intangible assets. Tax benefits were granted for five years (extendable) and the local authorities could waive their own taxes. Specific promotion and executive bodies were set up to ensure appropriate implementation of the ZUR scheme.

ZUR's results were mixed, as was to be expected, and depended on the severity of the problems in specific regions. In those with minimal physical, technological, economic and social potential, the ZUR incentives were insufficient for restructuring. In these areas, ZUR programmes were followed by Declining Industrial Zones (ZID) programmes, which were also medium term. They were prepared by the government and submitted to the EC for financial support. The EC established a strategy adapted to each region that emphasized the removal of bottlenecks and the maximisation of existing potential.

consumption, compared with 25 per cent for Western Europe. Energy use as a share of GDP is nearly twice the OECD average. The result is a degree of environmental pollution of both air and water that borders on ecological disaster. The World Bank has estimated that the overall income losses associated with environmental degradation are in the range of 2.5 - 3.0 per cent of GDP.

The Polish government has adopted an ambitious Environmental Policy and insists that considerations be factored into the restructuring process. The Policy, the first of its kind to have been developed in Central and Eastern Europe, sets out specific objectives in the short (3-4 years), medium (10 years), and long (25 years) term.

However, the worsening economic situation is making it even more difficult to achieve the Policy's objectives. Environmental considerations dictate the immediate closing of some plants, but short term economic and social considerations often dictate the contrary. Polluters often have a better-than-average financial situation, they constitute an important source of hard currency, and employees can form an effective lobby.

The movement of energy prices toward world levels and the need for Polish enterprises to adopt internationally-competitive process and product technologies will promote an industrial structure in the longer term which will exert less pressure on the environment. But this will not be sufficient for achieving rapid environmental improvement. Specific investments and regulatory measures also are needed.

The integration of environmental considerations into industrial policy design has two major implications.

First, industry need a clear and stable regulatory framework. Such clarity is urgently needed in connection with environmental liabilities which may be acquired in the process of privatisation and foreign investment, and which have to be taken into account when assessing the long term viability of state-owned enterprises. Similarly, standard-setting and enforcement need to be established on a transparent basis.

Second, environmental rehabilitation of heavy industries should not take place to the detriment of the development of lighter industries. The methods for financing environmental measures must be therefore carefully chosen. Financing arrangements based on pollution charges are appropriate, provided that the levels of charges are adequate to match investment requirements. Complementary solutions have been developed in certain regions of Poland, such as eco-banks and debt-for-environment swaps. The point to note is that public support to environmental rehabilitation should in no circumstances help unviable firms survive.

4. Sectoral restructuring and foreign direct investment

Poland is in no position to target specific industries for special support because most industries contain both promising and unpromising firms, and it is too soon to tell which industries are likely to become growth poles under private ownership. Industrial strategy, as argued throughout this report, should build on the capabilities of promising firms rather than industries. Moreover, no strategy will succeed if it resembles in any way the earlier economic over-planning. Nevertheless, transitional strategies are warranted in two areas.

First, they are warranted in sectors where foreign direct investment (FDI) is eager to invest, such as consumer-oriented industries. The aim of policy here should be to use FDI to train and develop the labour force, upgrade technological capability, and encourage competitive domestic suppliers of parts and components.

Second, in heavy industries with a history of over-investment and structural distortion, some sub-branches may maintain a residual comparative advantage. A strategy is needed to give broad direction for capacity cutting, redirection and reinvestment (in smaller modern facilities, for example), as part of the overall, longer term privatisation programme.

Foreign investment is both desired and feared. Concern about "skimming the cream off the top" could be minimised by negotiating inventive schemes with foreign investors. These schemes could include: joint assessment and planning of work structures, personnel counselling, job search and placement, preferential placement and job development for workers, special on-the-job training, and employee venture fund/entrepreneurship training.

A broad strategy is also needed to encourage linkages and sub-contracting arrangements with foreign firms. Polish industry needs to be encouraged to internationalise, but this does not simply mean exporting or being "original equipment manufacturers" for foreign firms. It means establishing a presence abroad to scan the world technological frontier and screen investment and partnership opportunities.

5. Procurement

The drastic decline in domestic demand in the last 18 months has made it imperative for Poland to introduce a new "procurement system", or set of rules according to which public agencies obtain goods and services from private firms. The procurement system must be completely reformed as a consequence of radical changes in political and economic institutions. Procurement has been classified as a medium-term measure because it takes some time to set up a sound procurement system. However, its formulation should begin at once. While complying with GATT rules, the system can constitute a major form of assistance to SMEs. It can also help achieve improved quality and standardisation throughout the manufacturing sector.

Every OECD country has a set of rules that regulate government procurement. These rules attempt more and more not to discriminate against foreign firms bidding for government contracts. It is premature, however, to worry about such discrimination in Poland, since Poland no longer has any formal procurement rules. It might even be argued that the lack of rules biases procurement in favour of foreign suppliers since foreign credit is mainly available to purchase imports. Poland could consider bridging procurement policy and foreign investment policy by encouraging joint bidding by Polish and foreign firms.

Notes and references

1. OECD, *OECD/CCEET Economic Surveys. 1991-1992 series: Poland, 1992.*

2. I. Grosfeld and P. Hare, *Privatisation in Hungary, Poland and Czechoslovakia*, mimeo, 1991.

3. A recent OECD study — *Vertical integration and competition policy*, 1991 — presents detailed arguments on this point.

4. *Biuletyn Informacyjny*, National Bank of Poland, No 16, 1991.

5. According to the Minister of Environment, enforcement of the environmental programme would require the shutting down of one-third of all Poland's industrial plants.

6. The IFO patent statistics are established on the basis of information from the European Patent Office, especially: the year of first application; the classification(s) of the invention according to the International Patent Classification (IPC); and the country of origin of the invention and the name of the company (or owner).

7. Patent application in a foreign country entails higher costs (application, checking fees, translation costs, patent solicitor fees) than domestic application. The expected economic return from the invention must therefore be higher.

8. In particular, the inflationary effect of the Japanese patent system is eliminated. Japanese inventions are only taken into account if the applicant companies expect the invention to comply with US and/or European standards with respect to novelty and degree of technical change.

9. Agriculture has generally played an important role in the process of industrial development. It is now widely agreed that the United Kingdom industrialised first because it developed its agriculture first. In the United States, agriculture was the "leading sector" that provided the resources for investment in industry and linkages to the processing of agricultural output. In the fast-growing East Asian economies — Japan, South Korea, and Taiwan — land reform redistributed land and resources to small holders; government policy sustained the reform by providing tariff protection to agriculture and by pouring investment resources into credit, irrigation, fertilisers, and machinery. The result was high productivity.

    By contrast, agricultural development in Poland has stagnated. According to DRC (Domestic Resource Cost) calculations, processed agricultural foods are among the most inefficiently produced products in Poland. This is so, because agriculture has been poorly managed, even though roughly 70 per cent of agricultural land was privately owned and land fertility is relatively high. Under the previous regime, private farms generally received fewer resources than state farms, agricultural prices were distorted, and subsidised inputs (say, of farm machinery) created excess demand. Moreover, some farms were too small to generate a marketable surplus. The crisis in Polish agriculture became so acute in the 1970s that Poland became a net importer of farm products. The negative trade balance between 1971 and 1980 reached over $4.5 billion — a dismal performance for a country that was Europe's bread basket as early as the 17th century.

Nonetheless, the situation of agriculture is not disastrous. While the DRCs of certain agricultural products are negative, those of others indicate competitiveness at world prices (cereals, sugar and confectionery products, beverages and tobacco). In any event, agriculture can play a significant role in Poland's recovery if appropriate policies are adopted. For one, privatisation is less a problem than in industry. For another, the Polish peasantry has demonstrated its ability to respond quickly to incentives. Given the potential of Polish agriculture and the importance of agriculture in industrial development, industrial restructuring and agricultural restructuring should be undertaken together.

10. See in particular Jan Winiecki, *The Polish Transition Programme at Mid-1991: Stabilisation under Threat*, Kiel Discussion Papers, No 174, Kiel, 1991.

11. See in particular *Structural Adjustment and Economic Performance*, OECD, 1988, and recent issues of the OECD Industry Committee annual review, *Industrial Policy in OECD Countries*.

12. See *Industrial Policy Guidelines in an Open and Competitive Environment: Guidelines for a Community Approach,* Commision of the European Communities, Brussels, 1990.

13. The importance of the firm rather than the industry as the appropriate unit of competitive strategy is emphasized by Michael Porter, *The competitive Advantage of Nations*, The Free Press, New York, 1990.

14. *Rynki Zagraniczne*, No. 90 (5303), Warsaw, 27 July 1991.

15. If, for example, a Polish woolen textile company wishes to borrow in dollars to export, the EDB can only lend it dollars at a 9 per cent interest rate if it imports wool. If the company buys its wool in Poland, the EDB cannot lend in dollars at 9 per cent. It would have to lend in zlotys at about 50 per cent.

16. A number of international conferences took place recently to dicuss the need and modalities of government support to SMEs'development in Central and Eastern European countries; two of them were sponsored by the OECD/CCEET: a Workshop in Lodz in April 1992, held at the invitation of the Polish Anti-monopoly Office; an Expert meeting in Moscow in April 1992, organised jointly by the governments of the Federation of Russia and of Japan.

17. "Challenges and opportunities facing small business in a global economy", Conference organised by the Federal Business Development Bank of Canada and the OECD, Montreal, 24-27 May 1992.

18. See *Regional development problems and policies in Poland*, OECD, forthcoming 1992.

Annex 1

Maps, supplementary charts and tables

Maps

General
(Charts 1.1 to 1.3)

Economic and industrial structures
(Charts 1.4 to 1.11 and tables 1.1 and 1.2)

Employment, wages and prices
(Chart 1.12 and tables 1.3 to 1.8)

Investment
(Chart 1.13 and tables 1.9 to 1.12)

Trade
(Charts 1.14 and 1.15 and tables 1.13 to 1.16)

Energy and environment
(Chart 1.16 and tables 1.17 to 1.21)

Map 1. **Territorial organisation of Poland**

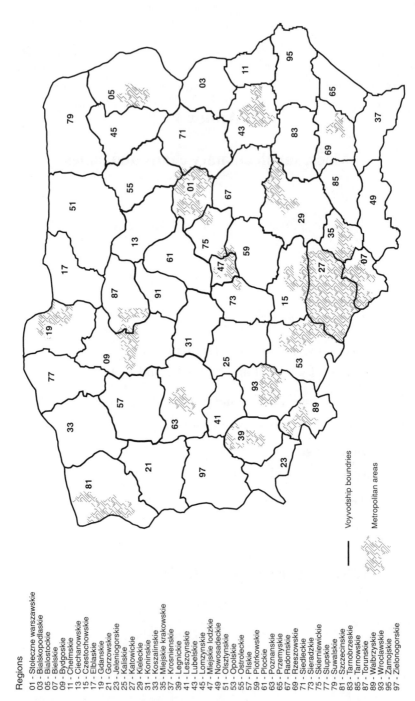

Voyvodship boundries

Metropolitan areas

Regions

01 - Stoleczne warszawskie
03 - Bialskopodlaskie
05 - Bialostockie
07 - Bielskie
09 - Bydgoskie
11 - Chelmskie
13 - Ciechanowskie
15 - Czestochowskie
17 - Elblaskie
19 - Gdanskie
21 - Gorzowskie
23 - Jeleniogorskie
25 - Kaliskie
27 - Katowickie
29 - Kieleckie
31 - Koninskie
33 - Koszalinskie
35 - Miejskie krakowskie
37 - Krosnienskie
39 - Legnickie
41 - Leszczynskie
43 - Lubelskie
45 - Lomzynskie
47 - Miejskie lodzkie
49 - Nowosadeckie
51 - Olsztynskie
53 - Opolskie
55 - Ostroleckie
57 - Pilskie
59 - Piotrkowskie
61 - Plockie
63 - Poznanskie
65 - Przemyskie
67 - Radomskie
69 - Rzeszowskie
71 - Siedleckie
73 - Sieradzkie
75 - Skierniewickie
77 - Slupskie
79 - Suwalskie
81 - Szczecinskie
83 - Tarnobrzeskie
85 - Tarnowskie
87 - Torunskie
89 - Walbrzyskie
93 - Wroclawskie
95 - Zamojskie
97 - Zielonogorskie

Map 2. Regional distribution of industrial production in Poland, 1990

Regions

01 - Stoleczne warszawskie
03 - Bialskopodlaskie
05 - Bialostockie
07 - Bielskie
09 - Bydgoskie
11 - Chelmskie
13 - Ciechanowskie
15 - Czestochowskie
17 - Elblaskie
19 - Gdanskie
21 - Gorzowskie
23 - Jeleniogorskie
25 - Kaliskie
27 - Katowickie
29 - Kieleckie
31 - Koninskie
33 - Koszalinskie
35 - Miejskie krakowskie
37 - Krosnienskie
39 - Legnickie
41 - Leszczynskie
43 - Lubelskie
45 - Lomzynskie
47 - Miejskie lodzkie
49 - Nowosadeckie
51 - Olsztynskie
53 - Opolskie
55 - Ostroleckie
57 - Pilskie
59 - Piotrkowskie
61 - Plockie
63 - Poznanskie
65 - Przemyskie
67 - Radomskie
69 - Rzeszowskie
71 - Siedleckie
73 - Sieradzkie
75 - Skierniewickie
77 - Slupskie
79 - Suwalskie
81 - Szczecinskie
83 - Tarnobrzeskie
85 - Tarnowskie
87 - Torunskie
89 - Walbrzyskie
93 - Wroclawskie
95 - Zamojskie
97 - Zielonogorskie

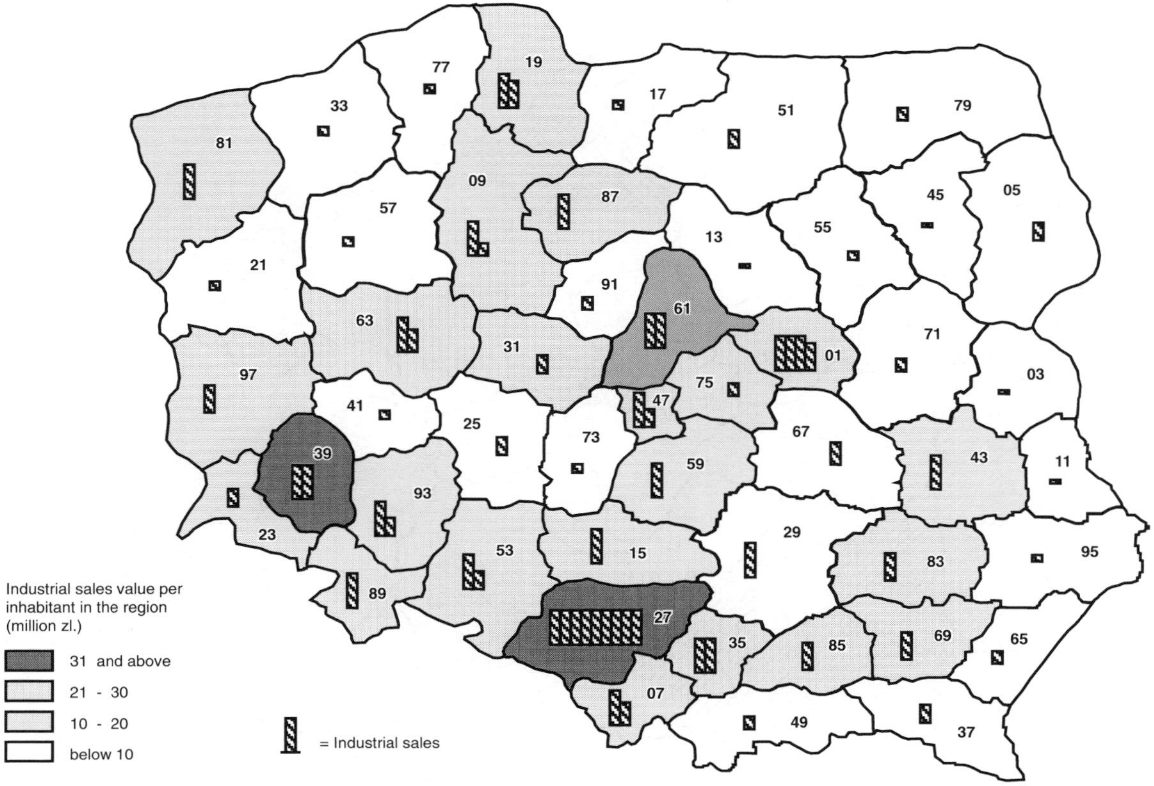

Industrial sales value per
inhabitant in the region
(million zl.)

31 and above
21 - 30
10 - 20
below 10

◨ = Industrial sales

125

Map 3. **Regional development patterns, 1991**

Regions

01 - Stoleczne warszawskie
03 - Bialskopodlaskie
05 - Bialostockie
07 - Bielskie
09 - Bydgoskie
11 - Chelmskie
13 - Ciechanowskie
15 - Czestochowskie
17 - Elblaskie
19 - Gdanskie
21 - Gorzowskie
23 - Jeleniogorskie
25 - Kaliskie
27 - Katowickie
29 - Kieleckie
31 - Koninskie
33 - Koszalinskie
35 - Miejskie krakowskie
37 - Krosnienskie
39 - Legnickie
41 - Leszczynskie
43 - Lubelskie
45 - Lomzynskie
47 - Miejskie lodzkie
49 - Nowosadeckie
51 - Olsztynskie
53 - Opolskie
55 - Ostroleckie
57 - Pilskie
59 - Piotrkowskie
61 - Plockie
63 - Poznanskie
65 - Przemyskie
67 - Radomskie
69 - Rzeszowskie
71 - Siedleckie
73 - Sieradzkie
75 - Skierniewickie
77 - Slupskie
79 - Suwalskie
81 - Szczecinskie
83 - Tarnobrzeskie
85 - Tarnowskie
87 - Torunskie
89 - Walbrzyskie
93 - Wroclawskie
95 - Zamojskie
97 - Zielonogorskie

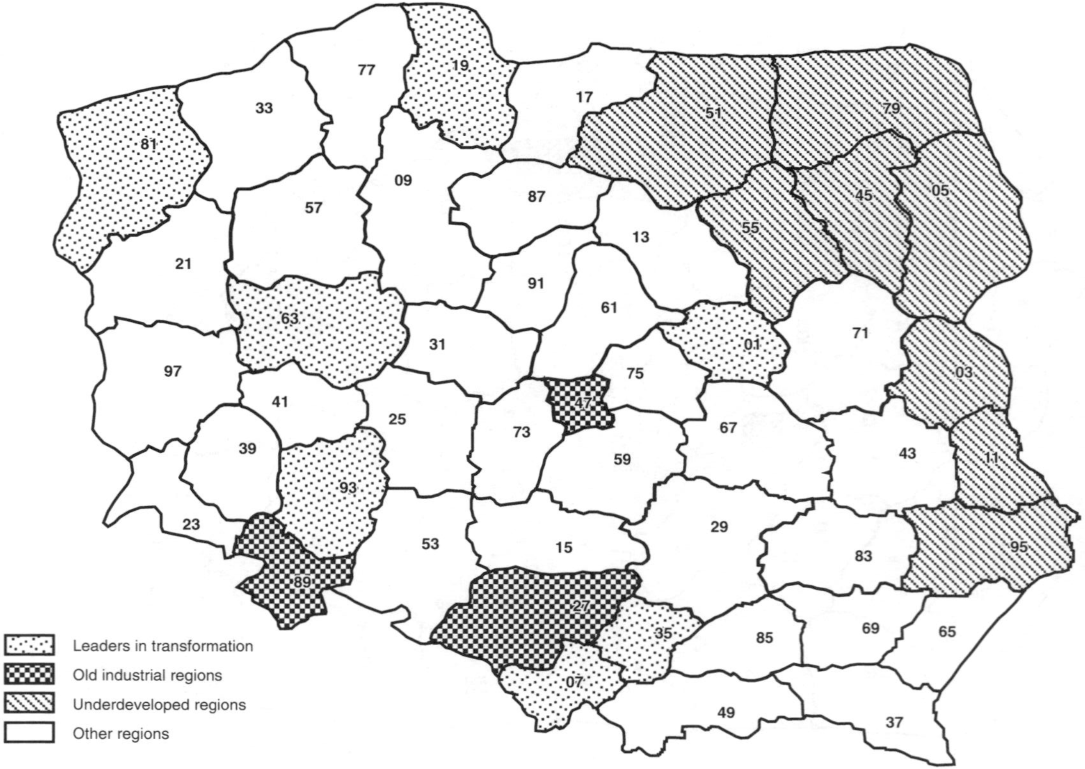

Leaders in transformation

Old industrial regions

Underdeveloped regions

Other regions

Map 4. **Regional structure of unemployment, 1991**

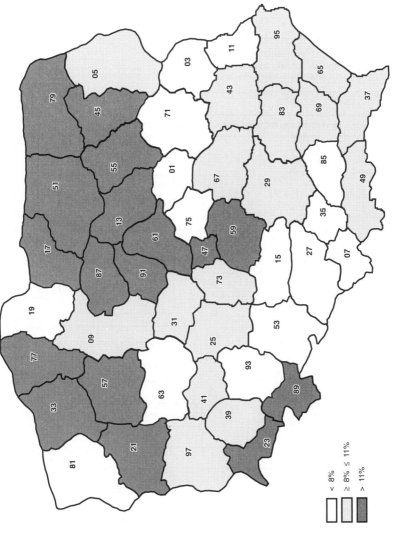

< 8%

≥ 8% ≤ 11%

> 11%

Regions

01 - Stoleczne warszawskie
03 - Bialskopodlaskie
05 - Bialostockie
07 - Bielskie
09 - Bydgoskie
11 - Chelmskie
13 - Ciechanowskie
15 - Czestochowskie
17 - Elblaskie
19 - Gdanskie
21 - Gorzowskie
23 - Jeleniogorskie
25 - Kaliskie
27 - Katowickie
29 - Kieleckie
31 - Koninskie
33 - Koszalinskie
35 - Miejskie krakowskie
37 - Krosnienskie
39 - Legnickie
41 - Leszczynskie
43 - Lubelskie
45 - Lomzynskie
47 - Miejskie lodzkie
49 - Nowosadeckie
51 - Olsztynskie
53 - Opolskie
55 - Ostroleckie
57 - Pilskie
59 - Piotrkowskie
61 - Plockie
63 - Poznanskie
65 - Przemyskie
67 - Radomskie
69 - Rzeszowskie
71 - Siedleckie
73 - Sieradzkie
75 - Skierniewickie
77 - Slupskie
79 - Suwalskie
81 - Szczecinskie
83 - Tarnobrzeskie
85 - Tarnowskie
87 - Torunskie
89 - Walbrzyskie
93 - Wroclawskie
95 - Zamojskie
97 - Zielonogorskie

Chart 1.1. **PRIVATISATION THROUGH COMMERCIALISATION**

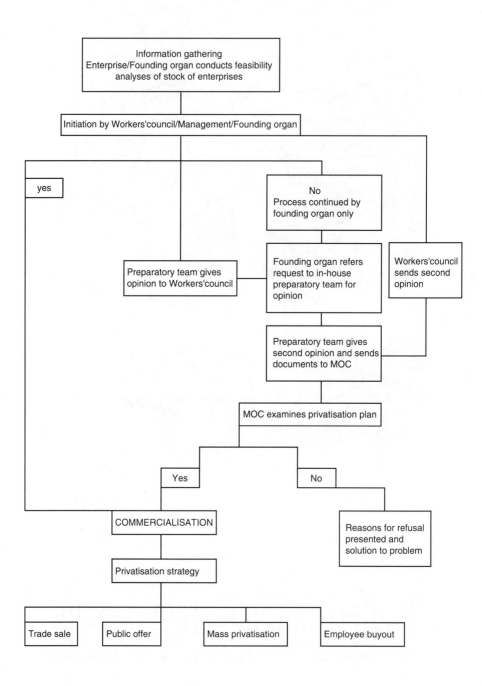

Source: Polish Ministry of Ownership Changes (MOC).

Chart 1.2. **PRIVATISATION THROUGH LIQUIDATION**

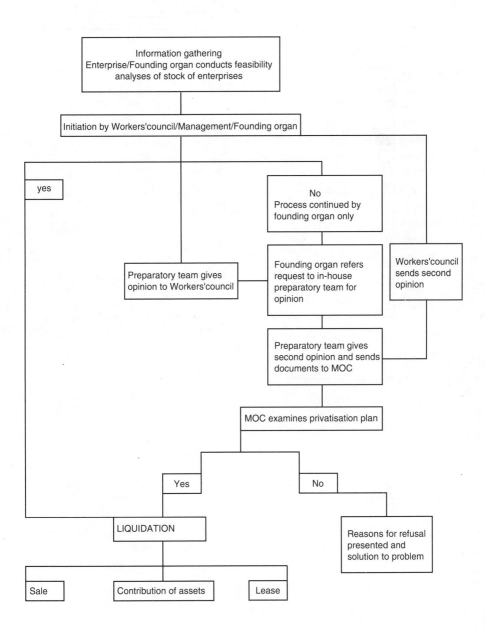

Source: Polish Ministry of Ownership Changes (MOC).

Chart 1.3. **MAJOR NATIONAL MILITARY BUDGETS, 1988**

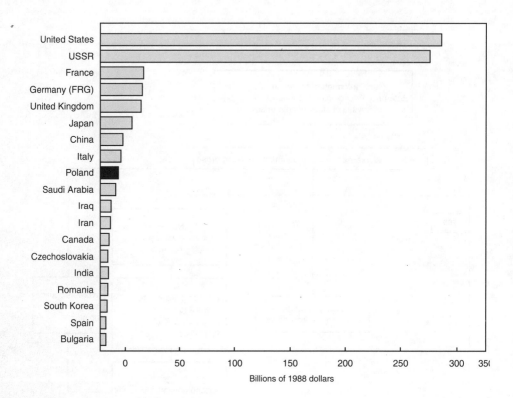

Billions of 1988 dollars

Source: US Arms Control and Disarmament Agency.

Chart 1.4.

Trend in GPD per capita
(Purchasing Power Parities; 1980 $)

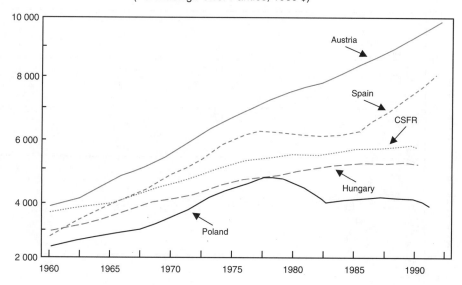

Source: CEPII.

Relative importance of major sectors
(%)

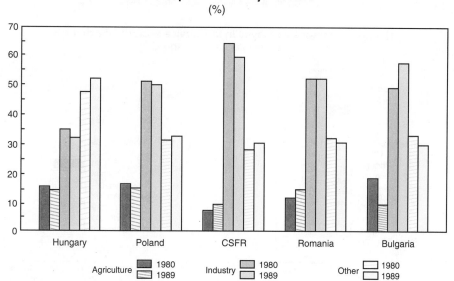

Note: The data for Hungary are based on the GDP for 1980 and 1988;
data for all other countries are based on the NMP for 1980 and 1989.

Source: UN, Monthly bulletin of statistics, July 1991.

131

Chart 1.5.

Employment in the service sector per capita GDP

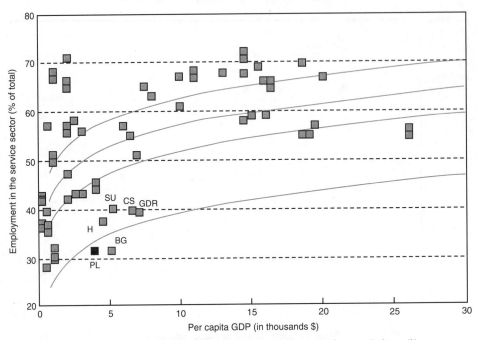

SU: USSR; CS: Czechoslovakia; H: Hungary; PL: Poland; BG: Bulgaria; GDR: Eastern Germany (before unif.).

Number of persons employed in the service sector in the mid-80s
(% of total employment)

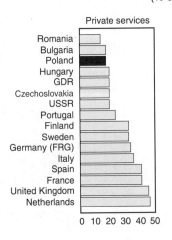

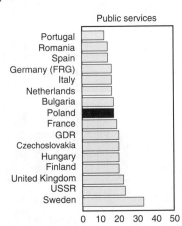

Source: Services in Central and Eastern European countries, OECD, 1991.

Chart 1.6. **ENTERPRISES OF THE SOCIALISED SECTOR (STATE-OWNED AND CO-OPERATIVES) DISTRIBUTION BY SIZE**

1989

(% of employment in socialised sector)

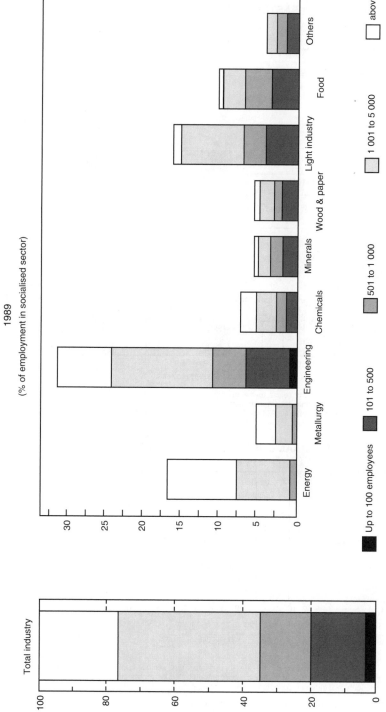

Source: Polish Ministry of Industry and Trade (Promasz).

Chart 1.7. DISTRIBUTION OF EMPLOYEES IN INDUSTRY BY ENTERPRISE SIZE IN CENTRAL AND EASTERN EUROPE AND IN OECD COUNTRIES [1], 1990

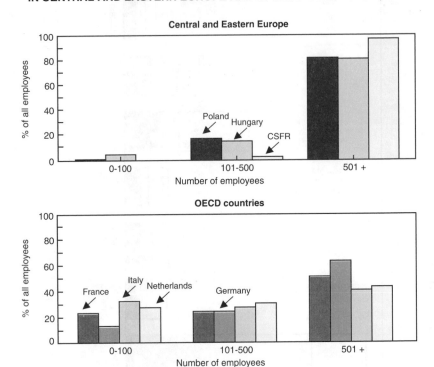

1. Industry generally refers to the mining, manufacturing and electricity, gas and water sectors. For the Netherlands, only the manufacturing sector is included. The reference year is 1989 for the CSFR, Hungary and Poland, 1988 for France and the Netherlands, and 1987 for Germany and Italy.

SECTORAL CONCENTRATION PATTERNS IN POLAND [1]

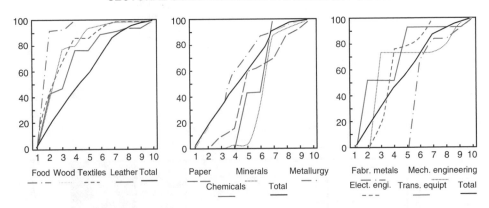

1. Calculations are based on the production share of the 4 largest firms in each sub-sector. X axis represents deciles of increasing concentration; Y axis represents cumulative sales. The more convex a curve is, the more concentrated a sector is.

Sources: OECD; Polish Ministry of Industry and Trade (Promasz).

134

Chart 1.8. **DETERGENTS INDUSTRY**

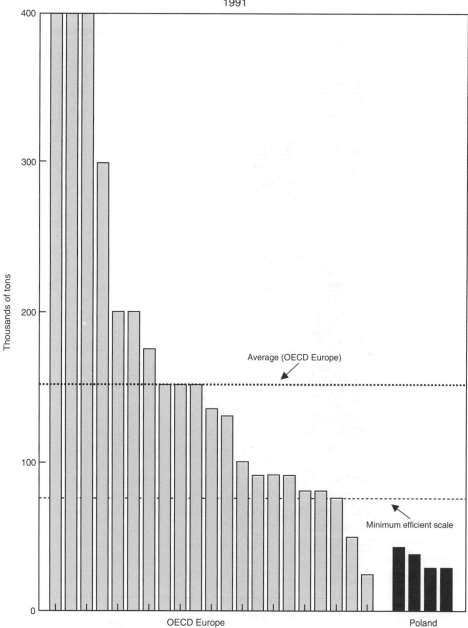

Annual capacity of major plants
1991

Source: Bain & Compagny.

135

Chart 1.9. **CAPITAL INTENSITY, 1989**

(Capital stock per employee)

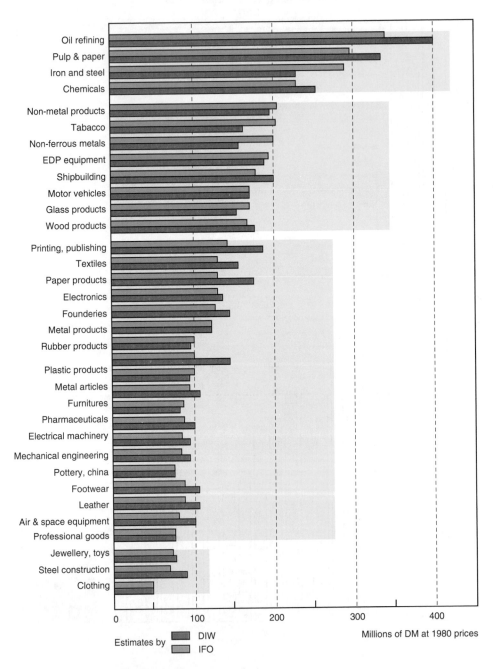

Estimates by ■ DIW
□ IFO

Millions of DM at 1980 prices

Source: OECD Trade Statistics, IFO calculations.

Chart 1.10. DEGREE OF COMPETITION FROM LOW-WAGE COUNTRIES
(Share of imports from non - OECD countries in total imports of the most developed countries)

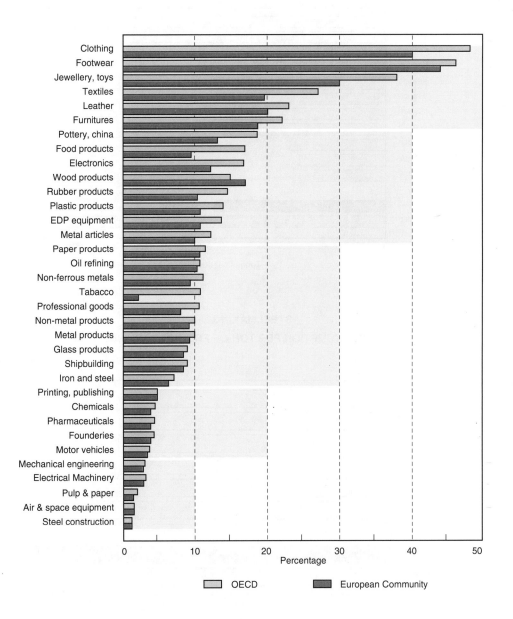

Percentage

☐ OECD   ■ European Community

Source: OCDE Trade Statistics; IFO calculations.

Chart 1.11. APPARENT CONSUMPTION PER CAPITA
FINISHED STEEL PRODUCTS, 1989

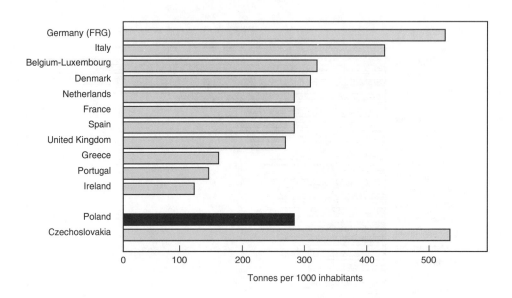

Tonnes per 1000 inhabitants

Sources: Eurostat; IFO.

STEELMAKING
FUEL CONSUMPTION PER TON OF PRODUCTION, 1988

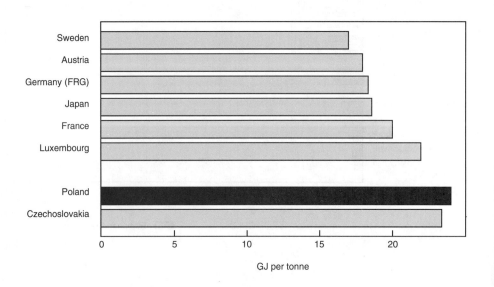

GJ per tonne

Source: UN Economic Commission for Europe.

Table 1.1. **Number and density of main telephone lines
in Central and Eastern European countries, 1990**

Country	Total number of main lines (in thousands) 1.1.1990	Density per 100 inhabitants 1990	To reach the average OECD density by the year 2000 (40 main lines per 100 inhabitants)	
			Number of lines (in thousands)	AAGR[1]
Poland	3 277.6	8.63	11 920	16.6
Bulgaria	1994	22.23	1 594	6.1
CSFR	2 226.4	14.26	4 018	10.9
Hungary	916	8.64	3 322	16.6
Romania	2 161.3	9.42	7 013	15.6
USSR[2]	33 991.1	12.01	79 249	12.0
Yougoslavia[2]	3 267.1	13.82	6 188	13.8
Total Eastern and Central Europe	47 833.5	11.87	113 304	12.9
OECD[3]	341 302.5	41.37	---	---

1. Average Annual Growth Rate.
2. On the basis of 1989 data.
3. Data for OECD : 1.1.1989.

Source : OECD.

139

Table 1.2. **Development of the private industrial sector**

Recent trends in sales and employment
Index. %

| | 1988=100 | | | | | % share | | | | |
	1988	1989	1990	1990*	1990**	1988	1989	1990	1990*	1990**
Sales										
Private sector	100	122	132	---	---	10.7	11.5	12.7	---	---
Socialised sector	100	98.6	74	---	---	89.3	88.5	87.3	---	---
Total industry	100	99.5	75.6	---	---	100	100	100	---	---
Employment										
Private sector	100	124.8	157.9	120.3	238.1	2.8	3.5	4.8	3.6	7.7
Socialised sector	100	96.9	87.8	91.8	80.2	97.2	96.5	95.2	96.4	92.3
Total industry	100	100.3	92	92.6	84.5	100	100	100	100	100

* January.
** December.

Industrial SMEs
Number of enterprises

| | End 1988 | | End 1989 | | End 1990 | | 1991 (1st quarter) | |
	Total	Industry	Total [1]	Industry	Total	Industry	Total	Industry
Incorporated [2]	1 275	---	11 693 [11]	2 769	29 650	6 416	33 830	7 077
Polonia firms [3]	689	---	841 [138]	731	862	739	870	748
Joint ventures	32	--	429 [69]	240	1 645	853	2 290	1 164
Unincorporated [4]	660 000	---	814 500 [<2]	---	1 135 600	248 300	---	243 900

1. In squared brackets : average number of employees per enterprise.
2. Joint stock companies and limited liability companies.
3. Small companies operated by foreign persons on the basis of the law from July 1982.
4. Sole proprietorships and partnerships.

Unincorporated industrial enterprises by sector
March 1991

	Metal	Electronics	Chemicals	Wood	Textiles	Clothing	Other	Total
Number of enterprises (%)	15.4	11.4	5.1	15.8	5.4	19.8	27.1	100

Sources : Polish Ministry of Industry and Trade (Promasz); M. Grabowski, *The development of the SME sector in Poland in the 80's,* 1991.

Chart 1.12. **COMPENSATION PER EMPLOYEE, 1990**

($ at 1990 exchange rate)

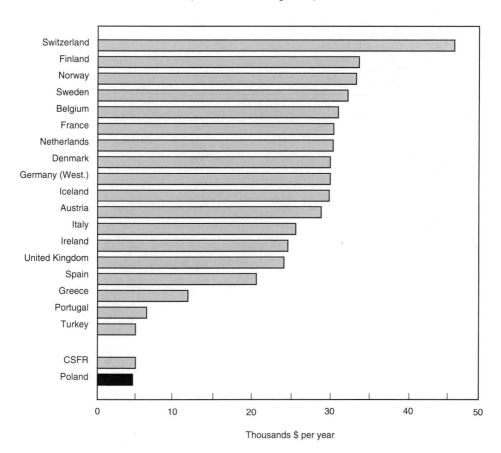

Thousands $ per year

Sources: OECD; IFO.

Table 1.3. **Employment in industry**

Sector	% change [1]				Thousands					Decrease 1990(I)-1991(VIII)		Share (%)		
	1989	1990	1991 I-III	1991 I-VIII	1990	1990 I	1990 XII	1991 III	1991 VIII	Thousands	%	1990 I	1990 XII	1991 VIII
Total industry	0.3	-8.2	-6.8	-7.3	3 856	3 979	3 632	3 657	3 455	580	14.5	100.0	100.0	100.0
Mining and quarrying	2.4	-11.5	-9.6	-10.0	507	530	484	473	453	85	16.0	13.3	13.3	13.1
Manufacturing	-3.8	-7.7	-6.4	-6.9	3 349	3 449	3 148	3 184	3 002	495	14.0	86.7	86.7	86.9
Energy	0.8	-5.7	-8.0	-7.2	603	625	579	572	560	70	11.0	15.7	15.9	16.2
Coal	2.0	-8.2	-11.1	-9.8	430	452	408	398	386	70	15.5	11.4	11.2	11.2
Fuel	-3.6	-0.3	-1.7	-1.1	54	54	53	53	53	--	--	1.4	1.5	1.5
Power	-2.2	1.8	0.7	-0.1	119	118	118	120	121	--	--	3.0	3.2	3.5
Metallurgy	-3.9	-4.7	-6.4	-7.5	195	200	187	186	177	25	12.5	5.0	5.1	5.1
Iron and steel	-4.5	-5.6	-7.4	-7.2	136	141	130	129	124	15	11.0	3.5	3.6	3.6
Non-ferrous metals	-2.3	-2.8	-4.0	-8.3	58	60	57	57	53	10	16.0	1.5	1.6	1.5
Engineering	-4.4	-9.4	-9.4	-9.6	1 216	1 269	1 117	1 138	1 041	240	18.5	31.9	30.8	30.1
Metal products	-2.9	-9.4	-5.3	-2.8	224	231	210	218	210	25	10.5	5.8	5.8	6.1
Machinery, non-electrical	-4.5	-10.8	-10.0	-10.6	385	403	351	358	322	85	21.0	10.1	9.7	9.3
Precision instruments	-11.4	-10.3	-11.7	-15.3	72	74	68	63	56	20	26.5	1.9	1.9	1.6
Transport equipment	-4.6	-8.5	-9.4	-7.2	301	314	278	284	268	45	14.5	7.9	7.7	7.8
Electrical and electronics	-3.2	-8.0	-11.8	-15.6	233	246	210	215	185	65	26.0	6.2	5.8	5.4
Chemicals	-1.0	-6.1	-4.5	-5.5	271	275	258	262	249	25	9.0	6.9	7.1	7.2
Mineral products	-6.0	-6.0	-2.4	-2.7	205	206	194	198	193	10	5.0	5.2	5.3	5.6
Building materials	-6.0	-6.8	-1.3	-1.1	135	134	128	130	129	5	3.5	3.4	3.5	3.7
Glass	-4.9	-5.4	-4.0	-4.7	47	47	44	45	43	--	--	1.2	1.2	1.2
Earthenware/ceramics	-7.7	-3.0	-5.2	-8.3	23	25	22	23	21	5	19.0	0.6	0.6	0.6
Wood and paper	-3.4	-9.7	0.9	2.1	208	211	197	210	205	10	4.5	5.3	5.4	5.9
Wood	-3.8	-10.2	2.5	4.2	164	165	156	170	165	5	3.0	4.1	4.3	4.8
Paper	-2.1	-7.7	-5.2	-5.8	43	45	41	40	39	5	11.5	1.1	1.1	1.1

142

Table 1.3. (continued)

Sector	% change [1]				Thousands					Decrease		Share (%)		
			1991			1990		1991		1990(I)-1991(VIII)		1990		1991
	1989	1990	I-III	I-VIII	1990	I	XII	III	VIII	Thousands	%	I	XII	VIII
Light industry	-3.9	-10.8	-11.8	-13.0	614	650	561	560	506	155	23.5	16.3	15.4	14.6
Textiles	-4.0	-11.1	-9.0	-19.6	290	317	255	251	224	95	30.0	8.0	7.0	6.5
Clothing	-4.0	-10.8	0.0	-2.9	195	197	188	193	176	25	12.5	5.0	5.2	5.1
Leather	-3.6	-9.9	-12.0	-13.0	129	135	117	116	106	35	25.0	3.4	3.2	3.1
Food industry	-2.2	-1.8	5.4	3.0	427	415	432	425	435	---	---	10.4	11.9	12.6
Other manufacturing	-2.0	-24.8	-14.1	-20.6	118	128	107	106	89	45	33.5	3.2	2.9	2.6
State-owned enterprises	-3.1	-9.4	---	---	3 670	3 837	3 351	---	---	---	---	96.4	92.3	---
Private enterprises	24.8	26.5	---	---	186	142	281	---	---	---	---	3.6	7.7	---

1. Compared to the same period of the preceding year.

Source : Polish Ministry of Industry and Trade (Promasz).

143

Table 1.4. **Employment according to education level, 1990**
Thousands, %

Sector	Total	Education level				Shares		
		University	Secondary	Elementary Professional	Elementary	2/1	3/1	4/1
	1	2	3	4	5			
Total industry	3 265.0	152.7	818.1	1 267.6	996.2	4.7	25.1	38.8
Energy	560.4	26.1	137.9	250.6	142.1	4.7	24.6	44.7
Coal	395.2	14.1	80.9	192.0	105.6	3.6	20.5	48.6
Liquid fuel	52.0	3.0	15.9	18.3	14.4	5.8	30.6	35.2
Power	113.2	9.0	41.1	40.4	22.1	8.0	36.3	35.7
Metallurgy	182.8	10.5	46.0	66.3	59.1	5.7	25.2	36.3
Iron and steel	126.7	7.2	30.5	44.7	43.7	5.7	24.1	35.3
Non-ferrous Metals	56.1	3.3	15.5	21.6	15.4	5.9	27.6	38.5
Engineering	1 019.0	61.1	289.2	397.6	263.1	6.0	28.4	39.0
Metal products	182.7	8.2	46.8	68.9	55.8	4.5	25.6	37.7
Machinery, non-electrical	326.5	20.2	93.3	131.5	79.0	6.2	28.6	40.3
Precision instruments	55.4	5.1	19.4	20.0	10.8	9.2	35.0	36.1
Transport equipment	262.6	15.2	71.6	107.3	66.6	5.8	27.3	40.9
Electrical and electronics	192.7	12.4	58.2	69.9	51.0	6.4	30.2	36.3
Chemicals	227.2	13.5	57.2	77.7	76.7	5.9	25.2	34.2
Mineral products	175.2	6.0	36.8	61.2	68.7	3.4	21.0	34.9
Building materials	112.5	4.0	24.9	37.9	43.9	3.6	22.1	33.7
Glass	40.9	1.3	7.7	14.7	16.7	3.2	18.8	35.9
Earthenware/ceramics	21.7	0.7	4.2	8.6	8.0	3.2	19.4	39.6
Wood and paper	162.9	4.6	33.5	58.9	63.2	2.8	20.6	36.2
Wood	125.2	3.4	25.0	47.2	47.7	2.7	20.0	37.7
Paper	37.7	1.2	8.4	11.7	15.5	3.2	22.3	31.0
Light industry	473.9	10.8	94.2	197.7	166.7	2.3	19.9	41.7
Textiles	245.5	6.9	50.9	90.5	94.5	2.8	20.7	36.9
Clothing	127.3	2.0	23.8	63.5	37.0	1.6	18.7	49.9
Leather	101.1	2.0	19.5	43.7	35.1	2.0	19.3	43.2
Food industry	362.9	15.4	96.9	123.2	122.9	4.2	26.7	33.9
Other manufacturing	99.9	4.6	26.4	34.3	33.6	4.6	26.4	34.3

Source : Polish Ministry of Industry and Trade (Promasz).

144

Table 1.5. **Average monthly wages
in the state and co-operative sectors** [1]

Thousands zlotys

	1983	1985	1987	1988	1989	1990
Total socialised sector	13.9	20.6	29.3	53.2	206.9	1 030.5
Material sphere	15.3	20.9	30.5	56.3	212.1	1 021.1
Agriculture	13.9	20.1	27.9	52.2	206.9	958.4
Industry	16.6	22.7	33.4	61.4	235.4	1 094.7
Building & construction	15.6	22.2	32.4	57.4	201.6	1 028.4
Non-material sphere	11.6	17.0	24.8	42.9	192.0	1 050.9
Education	10.9	16.6	23.0	37.9	190.0	1 057.7
Health	10.1	15.5	22.4	40.6	189.3	1 040.8

1. Excludes agricultural co-operatives ; includes wages, bonuses and other payments.

Average monthly wages in industry

	Thousands zlotys				Index, average industry=100
	1987	1988	1989	1990	1990
Energy					
Coal	61.7	107.5	368.1	1 670.2	153
Fuel	32.4	62.8	291.2	1 577.5	144
Power	33.6	60.6	253.9	1 231.9	113
Metallurgy					
Iron and steel	38.3	67.0	263.0	1 385.9	127
Non-ferrous metals	46.2	86.1	330.1	1 687.6	154
Engineering					
Metal products	27.9	50.4	198.6	944.1	86
Machinery, non-electrical	32.2	59.8	215.0	1 031.3	94
Precision instruments	31.3	59.3	205.4	948.0	87
Transport equipment	31.2	57.8	215.9	1 037.8	95
Electrical and electronics	29.3	56.1	207.9	960.0	88
Chemicals	29.7	58.1	223.8	1 072.0	98
Mineral products					
Building materials	28.1	50.4	196.3	937.8	86
Glass	28.0	53.2	202.1	950.9	87
Earthenware/ceramics	27.3	47.2	193.8	901.6	82
Wood and paper					
Wood	26.4	48.7	192.7	896.1	82
Paper	27.3	52.7	206.1	989.9	90
Light industry					
Textiles	27.9	51.0	200.3	872.0	80
Clothing	25.6	47.5	180.2	782.2	71
Leather	26.3	49.2	190.7	803.4	73
Food industry	27.0	52.6	214.5	1 006.4	92

Source : Polish official sources.

Table 1.6. **Labour cost comparison in spinning and weaving, 1990**

	Range of labour cost ($/hour)			
	above 10	5-10	1-5	below 1
Geo-economic areas	Most OECD countries	Most Southern European countries	Portugal and most newly industrialised Asian and Latin American countries	Poland, many Asian countries and most of the African countries
Sample of countries with distinctively lower wage than Poland	Egypt, China, Pakistan, Tanzania, Nigeria, Indonesia, Sri Lanka			

Source : OECD on the basis of data from Werner International.

Table 1.7. **Price developments**
% change

	1987	1988	1989	1990	1991
Retail price index	25.2	60.2	251.1	585.8	70.0
By type					
Food	21.7	49.4	320.1	674.7	48.0
Alcohol & tabacco	26.2	64.6	240.4	409.2	88.0
Non-food	26.1	66.4	228.3	593.3	76.0
Services	30.9	63.5	170.9	780.7	132.0
Producer prices					
Industry	26.6	59.8	212.8	622.4	48.0
Energy	31.4	70.2	138.3	933.0	80.0
Metallurgy	37.3	67.5	232.8	783.3	20.0
Engineering	23.8	55.5	203.2	553.6	35.0
Chemicals	30.1	62.2	195.0	676.0	40.0
Minerals	28.0	56.3	201.3	626.4	45.0
Wood & paper	30.3	48.3	232.6	559.7	45.0
Textiles & leather	24.4	57.2	224.0	408.3	45.0
Food industry	20.8	57.4	290.9	528.0	50.0

Source : Polish official sources.

Table 1.8. **Increases in nominal energy prices since January 1990**

	Date price increase implemented							
	January 1990	May 1990	Sept.-October 1990	January 1991	Overall increase Jan. 91/Feb. 90	May 1991	January 1992	March-April 1992
	Preceding period = 1.0							
Hard coal								
Industry	5	1.3	– "free prices" –		1.5			1.06
Household	7	1.5			1.5			
Lignite	2.5	–	– "free prices" –		1.5			1.07
Natural gas								
Industry	2.5	–	–	1.6	1.6		1.1	–
Household	5	2	–	1.8	3.6	1.4	1.7	1.04
Heavy fuel oil								
High sulphur	4.3							1.37
Low sulphur	4.1							1.37
Light oil (diesel)	1.9	– several times –			2			1.35
Gasoline	2	– several times –			1.7			1.19
Electricity								
Industry	3.8	–		1.15	1.15	1.25	1.15	1.1
Household	5	1.8		1.2	1.2	1.1	1.2	1.12
Memorandum item:								
Producer prices	2.1	1.01	1.1		1.4	1.02	1.03	n.a.

n.a. Not available.

Source: International Energy Agency, *Energy Policies-Poland,* Paris, 1990, p. 13 and data provided by the Polish Central Planning Commission.

Chart 1.13. DEPRECIATION AND INVESTMENT

(1989)

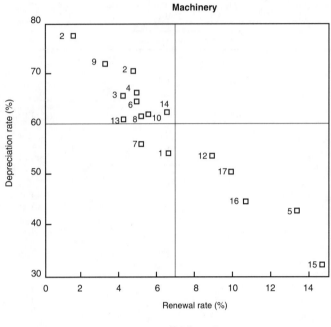

Machinery

Sectors	
Iron and steel	1
Non-ferrous metals	2
Fabricated metals	3
Machinery non-elect.	4
Precision instruments	5
Transport equipment	6
Electrical machinery	7
Chemicals	8
Building Materials	9
Glass	10
Ceramics	11
Wood	12
Paper	13
Textiles	14
Clothing	15
Leather	16
Food industry	17

Note: Renewal rate = Annual investment as % of assets' value

Total assets

Source: Polish Ministry of Industry and Trade (Promasz).

148

Table 1.9.   **Investment by type and decision-making entity**

%

	1987	1988	1989	1990
By Type				
Construction	58.0	56.8	57.0	56.9
Machinery & equipment	35.2	36.6	36.1	34.4
Of which				
Domestic	22.9	23.1	20.4	17.1
Imported	12.3	13.5	15.7	17.3
Of which	0.0	0.0	0.0	0.0
Rouble area	4.2	4.5	3.4	2.0
Non-rouble area	8.1	9.0	12.4	15.3
Other	6.9	6.7	6.9	8.8
Total	100.0	100.0	100.0	100.0
By decision-making entity				
Socialised sectors	83.9	84.8	83.4	80.1
State entities	11.2	10.3	7.3	6.4
Local authorities	10.4	10.6	9.9	7.1
Co-operative residential				
construction	10.4	10.0	11.2	14.0
Enterprises	47.5	49.8	51.6	50.1
Other	4.3	4.1	3.4	2.5
Non-socialised sectors	16.1	15.2	16.6	19.9
Total	100.0	100.0	100.0	100.0
Memorandum item :				
Share of construction in total				
investment	58	56.8	57	56.9

Source : Polish Ministry of Finance.

Table 1.10. **Fixed investment in industry**

Sector	% change, constant prices						Investment /sales %			
	1986	1987	1988	1989	1990	1991*	1988	1989	1990	1991*
Total industry	6.8	4.7	4.4	3.8	-18.0	-2.0	6.2	6.2	7.0	7.5
Mining and quarrying	-4.8	6.1	-7.6	-19.3	---	---	---	---	---	---
Manufacturing	9.5	4.4	6.9	8.1	---	---	---	---	---	---
Energy	7.3	-3.4	-6.2	-17.2	-11.0	---	12.1	12.7	9.6	---
Coal	-4.2	7.8	-8.1	-22.0	-34.0	---	13.2	16.7	12.2	---
Liquid fuel	28.6	-24.4	-13.2	-4.2	10.5	---	4.7	5.4	4.9	---
Power	9.3	-2.1	-1.3	-17.5	0.0	---	24.3	20.3	14.2	---
Metallurgy	6.4	-3.2	0.7	20.8	35.5	---	3.6	4.2	5.2	---
Iron and steel	14.9	-13.2	-4.8	25.0	70.0	---	3.3	3.7	5.6	---
Non-ferrous metals	-5.5	14.0	7.7	16.1	-5.5	---	4.0	5.0	4.4	---
Engineering	11.0	19.2	4.1	-3.8	-11.5	----	6.3	6.2	7.2	---
Metal products	-11.7	16.0	14.7	0.8	-24.0	---	5.0	4.7	4.6	---
Machinery, non-electrical	5.6	14.2	8.0	-12.3	-48.0	---	6.7	6.2	4.1	---
Precision instruments	20.0	26.8	19.8	29.1	-65.0	---	6.4	8.4	4.0	---
Transport equipment	19.3	23.0	-5.3	5.5	36.0	---	6.8	7.0	14.2	---
Electrical and electronics	26.2	20.9	3.8	-17.7	-16.5	---	6.2	6.0	5.0	---
Chemicals	-7.0	-0.1	12.4	19.1	6.5	---	5.7	6.6	7.4	---
Mineral products	2.1	2.4	0.0	6.0	-20.0	---	6.3	6.0	6.2	---
Building materials	4.0	-2.1	0.9	-0.5	-28.0	---	6.4	5.9	5.1	---
Glass	5.0	21.5	-3.0	46.3	0.0	---	5.0	5.8	8.5	---
Earthenware/ceramics	-14.0	15.4	-2.5	0.1	0.0	---	9.0	6.7	6.3	---
Wood and paper	8.1	2.2	26.0	18.6	3.5	---	5.5	5.6	7.8	---
Wood	8.0	10.4	28.1	30.9	-11.0	---	4.5	4.9	6.3	---
Paper	8.2	-7.2	23.1	1.1	20.0	---	8.1	7.7	11.0	---
Light industry	-1.2	4.2	25.9	18.8	-41.0	---	3.9	3.9	4.6	---
Textiles	2.7	-4.8	26.7	25.2	-42.5	---	4.6	5.1	5.7	---
Clothing	1.0	19.0	15.5	24.6	-37.5	---	2.6	2.9	3.8	---
Leather	-17.5	30.9	32.9	-7.1	-50.0	---	3.5	2.5	2.7	---
Food industry	9.2	13.9	19.0	38.5	-9.5	---	4.6	5.0	6.3	---
Other manufacturing	43.1	-0.3	-6.6	-11.0	-18.0	---	5.1	4.3	5.5	---

*First four months.

Source : Polish Ministry of Industry and Trade (Promasz).

Table 1.11. **Fixed assets in industry**

Sector	Price index 1989/1984		Fixed assets (end 1989)			Fixed assets/sales (end 1989)	
				Active part [1]			
	Active part [1]	Bulding	Total 10^9 zl.	Value	Share(%)	Total	Active part[1]
Total industry	11.3	8.8	153 816	69 092	44.9	1.49	0.67
Energy	10.9	8.7	45 776	16 479	36.0	3.98	1.43
Coal	11.9	8.6	18 713	6 595	35.2	5.19	1.83
Fuel	10.8	8.9	7 282	2 178	29.9	1.45	0.43
Power	9.6	8.7	19 260	7 246	37.6	6.64	2.49
Metallurgy	11.7	9.3	18 933	9 179	48.5	1.82	0.88
Iron and steel	11.2	9.1	13 284	7 086	53.3	2.10	1.12
Non-ferrous metals	12.2	9.6	5 411	1 900	35.1	1.35	0.47
Engineering	12.2	9.2	37 484	19 452	51.9	1.44	0.74
Metal products	12.0	9.1	6 655	3 600	54.1	1.35	0.73
Machinery, non-electrical	11.3	9.0	12 068	6 066	50.3	1.72	0.86
Precision instruments	10.7	9.2	1 149	592	51.5	0.82	0.42
Transport equipment	11.0	9.3	10 555	4 784	45.3	1.48	0.67
Electrical and electronics	17.2	9.1	6 972	4 409	63.2	1.26	0.80
Chemicals	11.0	8.7	14 792	6 953	47.0	1.59	0.78
Mineral products	9.8	8.8	7 591	2 908	38.3	1.89	0.72
Building materials	9.2	8.8	6 004	2 120	35.3	2.14	0.75
Glass	11.5	8.8	1 002	518	51.7	1.25	0.64
Earthenware/ceramics	10.3	8.9	520	207	39.7	1.30	0.51
Wood and paper	11.8	8.7	6 132	2 894	47.2	1.20	0.56
Wood	11.8	8.6	3 371	1 418	42.0	0.88	0.37
Paper	11.8	8.8	2 777	1 534	55.3	2.13	1.18
Light industry	10.5	9.1	9 161	4 905	53.5	0.72	0.38
Textiles	10.4	9.1	7 152	4 124	57.7	1.08	0.62
Clothing	11.5	9.1	952	404	42.4	0.30	0.13
Leather	10.0	9.1	1 038	400	38.5	0.35	0.13
Food industry	11.1	8.4	12 240	5 224	42.7	0.56	0.24
Other manufacturing	9.8	9.6	2 484	1 185	47.7	1.03	0.49

1. Machinery and equipment.

Source : Polish Ministry of Industry and Trade (Promasz).

Table 1.12. **Fixed assets, 1989**
Value, depreciation and investment

Sector	Total assets		Invest-ment	Renewal ratio (%)	Machinery and equipment		Invest-ment	Renewal ratio (%)
	Value 10⁹ zl.	Deprecia-tion (%)			Value 10⁹ zl.	Deprecia-tion (%)		
Total industry	153 816	45.5	6 343.6	4.1	69092	61.4	3356.9	4.9
Energy	45 776	44.9	1 462.3	3.2	16 479	56.3	559.6	3.4
Coal	18 713	43.7	596.8	3.2	6 595	54.8	314.0	4.8
Fuel	7 282	50.2	269.2	3.7	2 178	65.3	57.7	2.6
Power	19 260	44.0	596.3	3.1	7 246	55.0	187.9	2.6
Metallurgy	18 933	53.8	435.8	2.3	9 179	76.3	193.3	2.1
Iron and steel	13 284	55.9	234.7	1.8	7 086	77.8	104.3	1.5
Non-ferrous metals	5 411	48.4	201.0	3.7	1 900	70.7	89.1	4.7
Engineering	37 484	44.7	1 615.5	4.3	19 452	63.0	987.2	5.1
Metal products	6 655	46.5	230.7	3.5	3 600	65.8	151.8	4.2
Machinery, non-electrical	12 068	46.6	437.4	3.6	6 066	66.5	295.5	4.9
Precision instruments	1 149	35.5	115.1	10.0	592	43.3	79.3	13.4
Transport equipment	10 555	44.1	501.5	4.8	4 784	64.7	233.2	4.9
Electrical equipment and electronics	6972	41.9	330.8	4.7	4409	56.3	227.3	5.2
Chemicals	14 792	45.7	617.7	4.2	6 953	61.8	361.9	5.2
Mineral products	7 591	46.8	236.5	3.1	2 908	69.0	109.6	3.8
Building materials	6 004	47.3	163.2	2.7	2 120	72.1	67.6	3.2
Glass	1 002	47.0	49.3	4.9	518	62.2	28.4	5.5
Earthenware/ceramics	520	41.0	204.0	4.6	207	54.5	13.6	6.6
Wood and paper	6 132	43.1	287.6	4.7	2 894	57.8	191.5	6.6
Wood	3 371	39.9	186.9	5.5	1 418	54.0	126.6	8.9
Paper	2 777	47.1	100.8	3.6	1 534	61.2	64.9	4.2
Light industry	9 161	47.1	496.0	5.4	4 905	58.1	369.0	7.5
Textiles	7 152	51.9	334.2	4.7	4 124	62.7	266.5	6.5
Clothing	952	27.1	88.6	9.3	404	32.5	59.5	14.7
Leather	1 038	35.9	73.2	7.1	400	44.9	42.9	10.7
Food industry	12 240	39.3	1 082.7	8.8	5 224	50.2	517.1	9.9
Other manufacturing	2 484	42.1	103.5	4.2	1 185	55.6	66.2	5.6

Source : Polish Ministry of Industry and Trade (Promasz).

Chart 1.14. **POLISH INDUSTRIAL TRADE**

(%, 1988-1990)

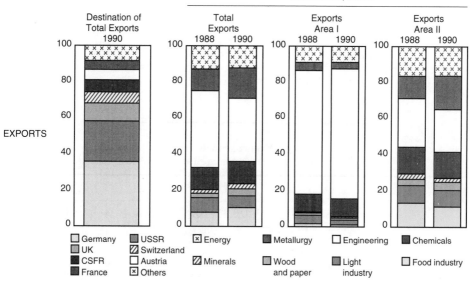

Sectoral composition

EXPORTS

Destination of Total Exports 1990 — Total Exports 1988 1990 — Exports Area I 1988 1990 — Exports Area II 1988 1990

Germany | USSR | ☒ Energy | Metallurgy | Engineering | Chemicals
UK | ☒ Switzerland | | | |
CSFR | Austria | ☒ Minerals | Wood and paper | Light industry | Food industry
France | ☒ Others

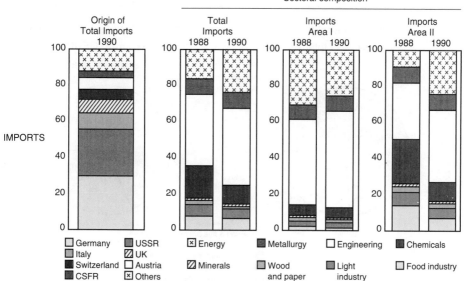

Sectoral composition

IMPORTS

Origin of Total Imports 1990 — Total Imports 1988 1990 — Imports Area I 1988 1990 — Imports Area II 1988 1990

Germany | USSR | ☒ Energy | Metallurgy | Engineering | Chemicals
Italy | ☒ UK | | | |
Switzerland | Austria | ☒ Minerals | Wood and paper | Light industry | Food industry
CSFR | ☒ Others

Note: Area I : Trade contracted in transferable roubles.
Area II : Trade contracted in hard currency, with currency clearing arrangements.

Source: UNIDO.

153

Chart. 1.15.   **POLISH TRADE WITH OECD COUNTRIES**
Exports, imports and trade balance
($ millions)

	1988	1989	1990	1991[1]
Exports	5 716	6 127	8 867	9 585
Imports	4 981	6185	7 707	12 645
Balance	735	-58	1 159	-3 060

1. January to July at annual rates.

Source : OECD.

Export growth
Ecus ; % change compared to the same period of the previous year

			1990				1991	
	1988	1989	Q1	Q2	Q3	Q4	Q1	Q2
Poland	13.5	15	13.8	20.2	27	37.2	24.5	8.7
CSFR	6.6	16.1	6.7	1.7	-2.2	0.7	15	29.5
Hungary	7.9	18.1	9.7	8.8	9.8	8.5	19.5	22.4

Source : OECD.

Export composition

(1989; % of total)

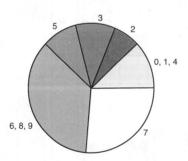

6, 8, 9

NTMs [1] confronting top 100 Polish export to OECD

(1989; % of total)

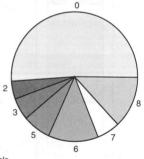

1. Non-tarif measures.

Sources: OECD; UNCTAD.

☐ 0 Food & live animals
☐ 1 Beverages & tobacco
■ 2 Crude materials, except fuels
■ 3 Mineral fuels
☐ 4 Animal and vegetable oils, fats and waxes
■ 5 Chemicals
■ 6 Manufactured goods classified by material
☐ 7 Machinery and transport equipment
☐ 8 Miscellaneous manufactures
☐ 9 Commodities and transactions n.e.s.

Table 1.13. **Exports of industrial goods**
Index, %, constant prices

	1971-1978		1979-1982		1983-1988		1989	1990	1991*
	Total for period	Yearly average	Total for period	Yearly average	Total for period	Yearly average			
Total industry	201	9.1	87	-3.5	149	6.9	-1.2	12.3	-3.3
From total:									
Energy	137	4.0	70	-8.6	120	3.1	-2.9	7.1	-8.2
Metallurgy	160	6.0	99	-0.3	140	5.7	-1.3	44.2	31.8
Engineering	250	12.1	100	0.1	145	6.4	1.7	-1.2	-22.2
Chemicals	197	8.9	84	-4.4	173	9.6	1.1	41.0	-10.8
Mineral products	212	9.8	56	-13.3	246	16.2	-7.9	29.5	22.4
Wood and paper	121	2.4	74	-7.4	205	12.8	-11.0	16.4	37.6
Light industry	221	10.4	68	-9.1	126	3.9	-18.9	2.6	-6.9
Food industry	139	4.2	60	-11.8	231	14.9	2.5	18.7	-5.9

*First eight months.

Source : Polish Ministry of Industry and Trade (Promasz).

Table 1.14. **Imports of industrial goods**
Index, %, constant prices

Sector	1971-1978		1979-1982		1983-1988		1989	1990	1991*
	Total for period	Yearly average	Total for period	Yearly average	Total for period	Yearly average			
Total industry	228	10.9	70	-8.7	154	7.4	1.6	-15.7	38.7
From total:									
Energy	227	10.8	81	-5.0	126	3.9	0.6	8.1	9.9
Metallurgy	163	6.3	63	-10.8	123	3.5	-6.4	-37.9	-4.0
Engineering	262	12.8	55	-14.1	201	12.3	0.9	-6.9	30.5
Chemicals	292	14.3	88	-3.2	141	5.9	-4.2	-37.7	60.8
Mineral products	159	6.0	59	-12.2	128	4.2	-3.7	-4.5	72.2
Wood and paper	151	5.3	80	-5.3	124	3.6	4.0	-39.8	113.2
Light industry	147	4.9	77	-6.4	201	12.4	24.8	-29.7	46.0
Food industry	229	10.9	120	4.6	135	5.2	11.8	-35.9	135.5

*First eight months.

Source : Polish Ministry of Industry and Trade (Promasz).

Table 1.15. **Imports in total domestic use and exports in total sales**

%

Sector	Imports in total domestic use					Exports in total sales			
	1978	1982	1989	1990	1991	1978	1982	1989	1990
Total industry	14.5	12.1	14.6	17.1	24.9	14.2	14.4	16.4	24.2
From total :									
Energy	14.7	12.5	14.1	19.2	21.9	15.0	11.3	11.8	16.2
Metallurgy	12.6	10.3	11.3	10.3	15.1	9.9	12.1	15.4	27.6
Engineering	28.9	20.4	25.4	30.9	43.9	27.1	30.5	29.4	37.3
Chemicals	20.5	19.6	19.8	19.8	30.0	15.1	13.8	17.4	32.6
Mineral products	6.8	4.8	4.9	6.1	11.0	6.2	4.2	7.7	12.7
Wood and paper	8.9	8.1	7.4	6.5	14.5	14.1	12.0	15.1	23.3
Light industry	7.3	6.9	11.6	13.0	20.9	23.8	20.2	15.2	23.4
Food industry	3.9	5.6	7.6	6.8	14.1	5.3	3.9	8.1	14.5

Source : Polish Ministry of Industry and Trade (Promasz).

Table 1.16. **Sectors representing more than three percent
of Polish exports to the OECD**
1985-1989

SITC	Products	OECD	EC	EFTA	United States	Other OECD
32	Coal, coke	15.26	13.20	32.27	---	---
84	Apparel	7.45	9.16	2.97	8.74	---
68	Non-ferrous metals	6.39	8.21	---	3.57	---
1	Meat	5.69	4.12	---	36.18	---
5	Vegetables, fruits	4.66	5.28	4.37	---	---
67	Iron and steel	4.24	4.43	---	6.36	3.88
3	Fish	3.39	2.99	---	4.53	14.55
24	Cork and wood	3.31	2.97	6.80	---	---
65	Textile yarn	---	---	---	4.20	5.07
33	Petroleum	---	---	3.16	---	6.19
66	Non-metal minerals	---	---	---	3.14	3.08
2	Dairy products	---	---	---	---	4.08
71	Power generating	---	---	---	---	9.45
0	Live animals	---	3.70	---	---	---
72	Spec. machinery	---	---	---	3.11	---
35	Elec. current	---	---	3.94	---	---
74	Gen. machinery	---	---	---	---	3.77
52	Inorganic chemicals	---	---	4.42	---	---
77	Elec. machinery	---	---	---	---	5.02
27	Crude fertilisers	---	3.31	---	---	---
69	Metal products	---	---	---	4.60	---
51	Organic chemicals	---	---	---	---	4.70
78	Road vehicles	---	3.25	---	---	---
79	Other transport	---	---	4.54	---	---
Agriculture		13.72	16.09	4.37	40.71	18.63
Chemicals		0.00	3.31	4.42	0.00	4.70
Iron and steel		4.24	4.43	0.00	10.96	3.88
Textile, apparel		7.45	9.16	2.97	12.94	5.07

Source : OECD.

157

Chart 1.16. **INDUSTRIAL POLLUTION, 1989**

Air pollution

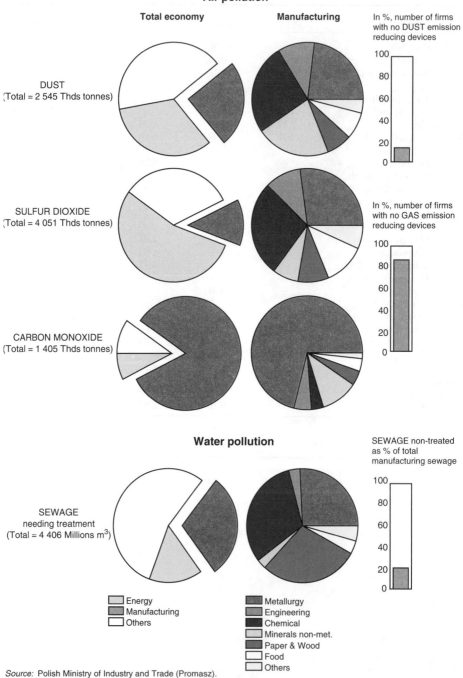

Total economy   **Manufacturing**

In %, number of firms with no DUST emission reducing devices

DUST
(Total = 2 545 Thds tonnes)

SULFUR DIOXIDE
(Total = 4 051 Thds tonnes)

In %, number of firms with no GAS emission reducing devices

CARBON MONOXIDE
(Total = 1 405 Thds tonnes)

Water pollution

SEWAGE non-treated as % of total manufacturing sewage

SEWAGE
needing treatment
(Total = 4 406 Millions m³)

Energy
Manufacturing
Others

Metallurgy
Engineering
Chemical
Minerals non-met.
Paper & Wood
Food
Others

Source: Polish Ministry of Industry and Trade (Promasz).

158

Table 1.17.   **Energy use in Poland**

Total final consumption by end use sector in 1988

%	Poland	OECD Europe
Industry	41	34
Transport	11	26
Residential, commercial, public agriculture and unspecified	46	37
Non-energy use	2	3
Total	100	100

Note : The comparaisons made in this table should be viewed as indicative only, as there is no single, generally accepted, methodology for calculating GDP in European Economies in Transition.

Source : IEA.

Comparison between Polish energy intensity and world energy intensity for selected industrial products, 1987

	Poland			Reference world energy index intensity	
	Direct energy consumption PJ/year	% share	Energy intensity Index GJ/t	GJ/t	Pol/world
Industry	1 682	100.00	---	---	---
Pig iron	244	14.51	15.50	11.80	1.31
Amonia from natural gas	82	4.88	39.00	32.40	1.20
Cement and clinker	87	5.17	5.30	3.10	1.71
Steel total	55	3.27	3.20 [1]	0.75 [2]	4.27
Sinters	31	1.84	2.00	1.70	1.18
Flot glass	8.3	0.49	18.50	11.90	1.55

1. Existing technological fraction : open hearth process 41%, BOF process 46%, electrical process 15%.
2. Technological fraction of electrical process 25% , BOF process 75%.

Source : Slawomir Pasierb, *Rational use of energy in Poland : present state and future tendencies,* 1990.

Table 1.18. **Emission of sulphur dioxide, selected countries, 1988**

Country	Emission (Thousands of tons)	Kg per person	Grams per unit of GNP
Poland	4 180	114	20
GDR	5 258	317	31
CSFR	2 800	179	24
Hungary	1 218	115	17
Bulgaria	1 030	115	21
Romania	1 800	80	19
USSR	18 584	69	10
France	1 226	22	1
Germany (FRG)	1 300	21	1
Sweden	214	26	1
United Kingdom	3 664	64	5
United States	20 700	89	4

Source : Worldwatch Institute.

Table 1.19. **Industrial air pollution, 1989**

Thousands of tons per year

	Emission of					Number of factories with very high pollution level	Including factories having emission reducing devices	
	Dust		Gas					
	Total	Fly-ash	Total	Sulfur dioxyde	Carbon monoxyde		Dust	Gas
Total economy	2 545.0	2 046.3	6 525.0	4 051.5	1 405.0	1 612	1 390	152
Total industry	1 452.7	1 136.0	4 905.9	2 690.6	1 267.2	1 297	1 128	150
Energy	806.0	785.1	2 870.0	2 165.3	110.8	164	149	6
Metallurgy	149.1	46.6	1 070.8	139.1	834.7	47	42	16
Engineering	67.1	41.4	160.5	58.6	58.6	296	279	46
Chemicals	171.9	138.4	302.9	144.3	35.9	114	99	51
Minerals products	138.1	18.6	193.8	40.5	124.1	167	140	10
Wood and paper	43.0	32.6	107.0	46.1	38.0	117	107	11
Light industry	22.8	22.0	67.1	31.8	20.7	127	103	4
Food industry	53.0	50.7	131.0	64.1	44.0	256	203	5
Other manufacturing	1.7	0.5	2.9	0.8	0.3	9	6	1

Source : Polish Ministry of Industry and Trade (Promasz).

Table 1.20. **Industrial air pollution, 1989**

Thousands of tons per year

Provinces	Dust		Gas				Number of factories	*Including* those with emission reducing devices	
	Total	Fly-ash	Total	SO2	NO3	CO		Dust	Gas
Warszawa	71.1	66.8	107.5	64.7	29.1	7.8	43	36	4
Bielsk Podlaski	1.2	1.1	4.2	1.6	0.6	1.8	18	15	---
Bialystok	14.1	13.3	23	17.2	3.9	1.3	18	16	1
Bielsko	62.8	56.8	48.2	27.0	7.9	8.7	37	34	5
Bydgoszcz	58.9	47.5	96.5	51.8	22.6	18.4	59	56	8
Chelm	21.3	2.0	39.6	7.0	4.4	27.9	19	15	1
Ciechanow	2.0	1.8	4.6	2.9	1.1	0.5	11	11	---
Czestochowa	31.7	8.2	68.3	18.4	6.3	37.2	63	56	5
Elblag	18.1	17.2	13.5	8.1	3.4	1.6	18	15	1
Gdansk	30.5	27.8	72.8	51.0	15.3	1.9	27	22	7
Gorzow	22.8	21.4	45.4	14.2	7.0	21.1	20	17	2
Jelenia Gora	98.1	96.9	246.9	210.3	18.3	12.8	45	38	4
Kalisz	6.7	6.6	25.3	7.6	2.3	8.1	25	23	2
Katowice	305.3	192.3	1 309.2	671.7	225.2	378.8	239	203	27
Kielce	21.5	6.2	63.1	38.4	13.9	9.1	60	53	1
Konin	70.0	66.5	172.3	146.1	21.7	4.3	15	14	2
Koszalin	2.8	1.8	5.9	2.9	1.0	1.8	10	9	---
Krakow	95.9	58.4	576.1	94.3	42.7	406.1	33	32	7
Krosno	4.3	2.6	23.1	5.5	2.9	13.5	21	19	2
Legnica	14.8	10.2	193.3	59.5	3.2	124.5	30	28	5
Leszno	3.0	2.9	7	2.9	1.4	2.6	14	14	---
Lublin	20.8	15.5	70.9	27.3	24.8	8.3	34	28	4
Lomza	5.2	4.6	13.1	8.5	2.4	1.6	24	21	---
Lodz	44.0	43.5	67	46.7	13.0	4.9	33	25	4
Nowy Sacz	2.4	1.8	8.1	2.7	0.9	3.1	9	9	3
Olsztyn	3.9	3.6	12.2	7.2	1.8	2.3	25	19	---
Opole	66.3	43.6	164.6	57.8	25.4	63.7	84	74	8
Ostrolenka	30,3	29,4	93.8	50.7	38.9	4.0	15	12	1
Pila	9.0	8.3	17.3	5.6	1.5	9.0	26	26	2
Piotrkow	42.0	40.4	509.1	419.4	68.6	16.9	46	38	3
Plock	4.8	3.8	108	68.9	5.7	21.4	27	22	2
Poznan	15.7	13.1	32	18.6	6.2	5.3	37	34	6
Przemysl	2.3	2.2	6	3.3	0.9	1.6	11	11	1
Radom	44.5	38.8	145.1	105.7	32.1	7.0	26	23	2
Rzeszow	4.1	3.8	19	11.4	5.4	1.6	22	20	2
Siedlce	2.8	2.3	8.2	3.7	1.1	3.4	20	11	---
Sieradz	8.7	0.9	8.1	7.2	0.8	0.0	5	4	---
Skierniewice	4.3	4.2	8	5.2	1.1	0.8	15	14	1
Slupsk	3.7	3.6	12.9	5.2	1.7	5.4	38	30	1
Suwalki	4.2	3.1	14.6	6.3	2.3	5.6	14	13	---
Szczecin	63.4	59.6	174.8	116.9	33.9	18.3	40	28	4
Tarnobrzeg	51.5	49.3	214.1	187.2	24.2	1.4	18	16	1
Tarnow	35.4	34.9	53.8	21.0	16.6	8.5	25	23	5
Torun	6.5	5.4	27.1	17.2	4.7	3.1	40	35	5
Walbrzych	29.3	23.4	38.6	18.3	5.7	8.7	52	41	6
Wloclawek	9.7	8.8	23.7	13.4	5.3	4.2	18	13	1
Wroclaw	30.7	27.4	64.8	37.0	18.0	4.3	44	40	4
Zamosc	2.3	2.2	12.9	5.4	1.6	4.6	12	12	---
Zielona Gora	8.5	7.2	39.3	9.5	3.7	26.0	27	22	3
Poland	1 513.3	1 192.9	5 112.6	2 790.3	781.9	1 335.0	1612	1390	152

Source : Polish Ministry of Industry and Trade (Promasz).

161

Table 1.21. **Industrial water pollution, 1989**

Millions of m³ per year

	Sewage total	*Including* Cooling water	Needing waste treatment	*Including* Waste treated	*Including* Waste untreated	Number of factories
Total economy	12 300	7 860	4 406	2 856	1 550	5 000
Total industry	9 828	7 860	1 962	1 517	445	2 953/1 819 [1]
Energy	7 942	7 345	653	513	140	150
Metallurgy	387	28	323	206	117	45
Engineering	91	22	68	55	13	270
Chemicals	839	394	434	343	91	139
Minerals products	79	8	72	60	12	223
Wood and paper products	261	21	337	199	38	103
Light industry	31	3	26	20	6	100
Food industry	130	32	92	75	17	544
Other manufacturing	62	8	57	46	11	45

1. Factories dumping industrial sewage needing waste treatment.

Source : Polish Ministry of Industry and Trade (Promasz).

Annex 2

Detailed statistics
on the industrial structure
of Poland

Table 2.1. **Industrial sales and concentration**

Sales at current prices
Production concentration ratio = sales of the 4 biggest producers as % of total sales

Classifi-cation	Product	Sales						Concen-tration (%)	
		Total (10^9 zlotys)			Share (%)				
		1988	1989	1990	1988	1989	1990	1989	1990
01-28	Total industry	28 987	88 299	478 309	100.0	100.0	100.0		
01-03	Energy	4 545	10 245	84 739	15.7	11.6	17.7		
01	Coal and briquets	1 780	2 817	21 171	6.1	3.2	4.4		
011-013	Hard coal	1 617	2 417	18 435	5.6	2.7	3.9	13.5	13.4
014-015	Brown coal	136	400	2737	0.5	0.5	0.6	99.7	100.0
02	Fuel	1 838	4 396	33 989	6.3	5.0	7.1		
021	Coke	348	631	6 638	1.2	0.7	1.4	85.2	91.1
022	Gas	336	697	5 379	1.2	0.8	1.1	68.4	69.0
023	Crude petroleum and natural gas	18	47	361	0.1	0.1	0.1	98.8	98.2
024	Liquid fuel and other petroleum products	1 135	3 020	21 609	3.9	3.4	4.5	76.4	78.3
03	Power	927	3 033	29 579	3.2	3.4	6.2	24.1	22.5
04-05	Metallurgy	3 189	10 193	70 758	11.0	11.5	14.8		
04	Iron and steel	1 824	6 147	42 846	6.3	7.0	9.0		
041	Ores	66	222	1 847	0.2	0.3	0.4	100.0	100.0
042	Pig iron and ferroalloys	94	318	2 558	0.3	0.4	0.5	61.6	66.6
043	Crude steel	47	159	1 045	0.2	0.2	0.2		
044	Semi-finished, hot rolled products	208	524	3 469	0.7	0.6	0.7	59.0	60.1
045	Hot rolled finished products	826	2 782	20 974	2.8	3.2	4.4		
046	Pipes	151	568	3 316	0.5	0.6	0.7	66.9	64.6
047	Cold rolled products	307	1 223	6 959	1.1	1.4	1.5	76.3	79.3
048	Forging products	123	337	2 491	0.4	0.4	0.5	34.9	35.5
05	Non-ferrous products	1 365	4 046	27 913	4.7	4.6	5.8		
051	Ores	310	614	6 189	1.1	0.7	1.3	67.9	69.2
052	Scraps	14	42	309	0.0	0.0	0.1	90.2	88.9
053	Metallurgical products	547	1761	13 601	1.9	2.0	2.8		
054	Metal ceramics products	16	62	211	0.1	0.1	0.0		
055	Rolled products	246	893	4 650	0.8	1.0	1.0	51.1	56.2
056	Extruded and drawned products	103	355	1 984	0.4	0.4	0.4		
057	Forging products	3	8	52	0.0	0.0	0.0		
058	Others	125	310	913	0.4	0.4	0.2		
06-11	Engineering	6 877	20 687	104 082	23.7	23.4	21.8		
06	Metal products	1 331	4 072	21 628	4.6	4.6	4.5		
061	Foundry products	349	1 024	5 855	1.2	1.2	1.2	15.5	19.3
062	Metal structures	159	468	3 103	0.5	0.5	0.6	46.5	48.8

Table 2.1 (continued)

Classifi-cation	Product	Total (10^9 zlotys)			Share (%)			Concen-tration (%)	
		1988	1989	1990	1988	1989	1990	1989	1990
063	Bearings	71	262	1 370	0.2	0.3	0.3	91.1	92.1
064	Metal tools	99	264	1 357	0.3	0.3	0.3	39.2	44.6
065	Metal goods for industrial use	380	1 105	5 502	1.3	1.3	1.2	42.4	16.5
067	Metal goods for household	269	942	4 408	0.9	1.1	0.9	42.5	43.7
07-08	Machinery	1 972	5 534	28 282	6.8	6.3	5.9		
071	Boilers, turbines, engines	354	1 095	5 230	1.2	1.2	1.1	38.1	37.5
072	For mining industry	287	745	4 041	1.0	0.8	0.8	37.6	37.0
073	For metallurgy and foundry	42	117	859	0.1	0.1	0.2	54.8	59.4
074	Metal-working machinery	136	420	1957	0.5	0.5	0.4	28.1	33.3
075	For chemistry	43	120	777	0.1	0.1	0.2	39.9	45.1
076	For building materials	24	75	348	0.1	0.1	0.1	65.1	66.8
077	For light industry	54	164	595	0.2	0.2	0.1	54.8	51.5
078	For food industry	60	194	958	0.2	0.2	0.2	30.1	25.0
079	For wood and paper industry	76	238	1 170	0.3	0.3	0.2	30.4	30.3
081	For construction	149	426	2 582	0.5	0.5	0.5	52.6	64.9
082	For agriculture	220	667	2 932	0.8	0.8	0.6	35.6	39.9
084	For trade and storage	38	322	1 322	0.1	0.4	0.3	75.0	63.2
085	Cranes and other transport equipment	258	333	1 663	0.9	0.4	0.3	27.0	30.7
087	Pumps, ventilators, other general purpose devices	213	593	3 740	0.7	0.7	0.8	20.9	27.1
09	Precision instruments	384	1 066	4504	1.3	1.2	0.9		
091	Controlling equipment	63	179	1 050	0.2	0.2	0.2	37.7	40.1
092	Computers & data processing machines	144	380	1 325	0.5	0.4	0.3	71.8	76.0
093	Office and calculation equipment	12	49	124	0.0	0.1	0.0	87.2	93.9
094	Measuring equipment	100	281	1 240	0.3	0.3	0.3	26.8	31.9
095.096	Optical goods	23	62	234	0.1	0.1	0.0	82.1	59.8
097	Medical equipment	33	102	470	0.1	0.1	0.1	64.4	62.1
10	Transport equipment	1 720	5 133	26 260	5.9	5.8	5.5		
101	For railroad	174	441	4 353	0.6	0.5	0.9	52.8	68.2
102	Motor vehicles	958	2 989	14 634	3.3	3.4	3.1	56.5	59.1
103	Tractors (agricultural)	180	429	2 015	0.6	0.5	0.4	79.6	83.7
104	Motorcycles and bicycles	55	218	880	0.2	0.2	0.2	86.3	85.0
105	Ships	250	755	3 122	0.9	0.9	0.7	71.8	59.3
106	Aircraft	80	246	986	0.3	0.3	0.2	94.3	93.4
107	Containers	13	29	141	0.0	0.0	0.0	80.0	82.0
11	Electrical and electronic apparatus	1 470	4 883	23 407	5.1	5.5	4.9		
111-113	Electrical machines and apparatus	795	2 606	14 333	2.7	3.0	3.0		
111	Motors, transformers	273	790	4 679	0.9	0.9	1.0	29.1	30.8
112	Cables and wires	232	890	5 021	0.8	1.0	1.0	82.5	80.4
113	Electricity supply	290	925	4 633	1.0	1.0	1.0	24.4	26.4
115	Electronics and telecommunication	673	2 274	9 061	2.3	2.6	1.9	29.2	29.8

Table 2.1 (continued)

Classifi- cation	Product	Sales						Concen- tration (%)	
		Total (10^9 zlotys)			Share (%)				
		1988	1989	1990	1988	1989	1990	1989	1990
12-13	Chemicals	2 975	8 650	52 925	10.3	9.8	11.1		
121	Sulphur, salt and other crude	179	558	3 484	0.6	0.6	0.7	91.6	90.9
122	Inorganic products	180	555	4 313	0.6	0.6	0.9	44.2	46.3
123	Fertilizers	224	620	3 799	0.8	0.7	0.8	58.2	72.2
124	Organic products	447	1 181	9 031	1.5	1.3	1.9	40.2	46.0
126	Plastics	229	683	5 389	0.8	0.8	1.1	67.0	73.1
127	Chemical fibres	170	553	2 862	0.6	0.6	0.6	81.9	88.0
128	Chemicals for industry	86	302	1 592	0.3	0.3	0.3	58.2	51.3
131	Paints	194	621	3 209	0.7	0.7	0.7	52.7	41.6
132	Soaps, detergents, cosmetics	240	619	3 136	0.8	0.7	0.7	37.3	40.2
133	Specialized chemicals	141	428	2 666	0.5	0.5	0.6	31.0	29.7
134	Pharmaceuticals	259	649	3 925	0.9	0.7	0.8	45.9	47.3
135	Herbal products	37	103	527	0.1	0.1	0.1	59.9	70.9
136	Plastic products	325	1 012	5 487	1.1	1.1	1.1	23.0	24.4
137	Rubber products	258	753	3460	0.9	0.9	0.7	61.6	60.0
14-16	Minerals	1 057	3 220	17 641	3.6	3.6	3.7		
14	Building materials	768	2 181	12 650	2.6	2.5	2.6		
141	Mineral crudes, non-metallic	150	398	2 032	0.5	0.5	0.4	25.7	21.1
142	Cement	158	503	3 116	0.5	0.6	0.7	40.6	39.4
143	Lime and gypsum products	43	121	775	0.1	0.1	0.2	62.7	62.4
144	Bricks and tiles, made of clay	80	242	1 000	0.3	0.3	0.2	30.0	27.3
145	Concrete products	157	422	2 669	0.5	0.5	0.6	15.6	13.0
146	Insulation materials	94	224	1 177	0.3	0.3	0.2	46.9	46.6
147	Refractory materials	75	240	1 692	0.3	0.3	0.4	58.8	59.2
148	Others	11	32	187	0.0	0.0	0.0		
15	Glass	209	726	3 651	0.7	0.8	0.8		
151	For building	39	155	869	0.1	0.2	0.2	68.1	72.8
152.153	For industry and household	93	310	1 582	0.3	0.4	0.3	38.2	39.3
154	Bottles and other containers	76	261	1 199	0.3	0.3	0.3	47.8	58.2
16	Ceramic products	80	312	1 340	0.3	0.4	0.3		
161	Porcelain and similar	41	143	697	0.1	0.2	0.1	47.1	47.6
162	Stonewares	12	48	215	0.0	0.1	0.0	78.1	84.6
163	Faience goods	27	119	421	0.1	0.1	0.1	82.0	80.4
17-18	Wood and paper	1 255	4 150	20 608	4.3	4.7	4.3		
17	Wood products	829	2 818	12 894	2.9	3.2	2.7		
171	Sawnwood	174	622	3 268	0.6	0.7	0.7	21.8	22.4
172	Boards, veneers and plywood	117	419	2 009	0.4	0.5	0.4	30.4	36.5
173	Materials for building	71	283	1 045	0.2	0.3	0.2	47.3	55.7
174	Furnitures	394	1 253	5 578	1.4	1.4	1.2	13.4	15.5
175	Packages	15	50	264	0.1	0.1	0.1	30.9	32.7
176	Matches	12	35	118	0.0	0.0	0.0	96.7	96.8

Table 2.1 (continued)

Classifi-cation	Product	Sales						Concen-tration (%)	
		Total (10^9 zlotys)			Share (%)				
		1988	1989	1990	1988	1989	1990	1989	1990
177	Others	40	146	577	0.1	0.2	0.1	61.5	68.0
18	Paper products	426	1 332	7 714	1.5	1.5	1.6		
181	Cellulose, paper and paperboards	207	690	4 261	0.7	0.8	0.9	59.8	63.6
182	Goods made of paper	208	614	3 354	0.7	0.7	0.7	35.7	42.7
19-22	Light industry	3 329	10 810	34 096	11.5	12.2	7.1		
19-20	Textiles	1 840	5 971	19 015	6.3	6.8	4.0		
191	Cotton woven fabrics (or similar)	552	1 794	5 074	1.9	2.0	1.1	24.8	26.2
192	Wool woven fabrics (or similar)	348	1 102	3 182	1.2	1.2	0.7	20.4	21.4
193	Fabrics made of bast fibres	77	259	598	0.3	0.3	0.1	34.4	35.4
194	Silk textiles	71	267	923	0.2	0.3	0.2	62.2	64.4
195	Tapestry	137	450	1 877	0.5	0.5	0.4	41.5	41.1
196	Cordage, rope and twine	30	120	335	0.1	0.1	0.1	83.3	79.0
201.203	Knittings and stockings	448	1 450	4 811	1.5	1.6	1.0	14.8	16.4
202	Goods made of felt	68	217	1 213	0.2	0.2	0.3	45.4	49.9
206	Non-weaved textiles	46	150	410	0.2	0.2	0.1	61.2	58.5
207	Others	56	141	537	0.2	0.2	0.1	34.4	42.6
21	Wearing apparels	745	2 289	6 911	2.6	2.6	1.4		
211	Clothes and underwear	461	1 442	4 550	1.6	1.6	1.0	14.9	16.7
218	Bed linen, articles	282	846	2342	1.0	1.0	0.5	13.1	20.7
22	Leather products	744	2 50	8 169	2.6	2.9	1.7		
221	Leather	164	559	1 849	0.6	0.6	0.4	28.4	27.4
222	Footwear	407	1 465	5 040	1.4	1.7	1.1	22.7	25.1
223	Furs	82	259	598	0.3	0.3	0.1	38.7	52.1
227	Other leather goods	87	260	665	0.3	0.3	0.1	17.7	17.7
23-25	Food products	5 165	18 759	86 908	17.8	21.2	18.2		
231.232	Meat and meat products	1 014	4 008	19 727	3.5	4.5	4.1	13.6	12.5
233	Poultry, eggs and products	216	655	3 141	0.7	0.7	0.7	27.5	24.5
234	Fish and products	156	447	2 735	0.5	0.5	0.6	73.5	76.4
235	Milk and diary products	675	2 719	10 413	2.3	3.1	2.2	4.8	5.1
241	Flour, cereal, macaroni	185	760	4 158	0.6	0.9	0.9	19.7	18.4
242	Bread and baker's wares	31	141	1 048	0.1	0.2	0.2	67.9	58.5
243	Sugar	275	1762	7 419	0.9	2.0	1.6	51.4	11.1
244	Alcoholic beverages	1 285	3 547	15 668	4.4	4.0	3.3	41.7	36.4
245	Potatoes and products	52	216	664	0.2	0.2	0.1	53.3	54.8
246	Fruits, vegetables and products	205	703	2 699	0.7	0.8	0.6	18.5	18.8
247	Wine and honey	129	453	1 297	0.4	0.5	0.3	19.7	16.4
248	Beer	246	731	3 940	0.8	0.8	0.8	33.9	36.0
249	Vegetable oils	104	394	2 240	0.4	0.4	0.5	60.5	63.3
251	Cakes, chocolates and sweets	252	970	4 198	0.9	1.1	0.9	34.4	37.3
252	Food concentrates	64	226	978	0.2	0.3	0.2	51.2	62.1
253	Soft drinks	35	96	604	0.1	0.1	0.1	37.7	37.1
254	Other food	57	175	752	0.2	0.2	0.2	19.8	23.2

Table 2.1 (Continued)

Classifi-cation	Product	Sales						Concen-tration (%)	
		Total (10⁹ zlotys)			Share (%)				
		1988	1989	1990	1988	1989	1990	1989	1990
255	Tobacco, cigarettes	184	754	5 225	0.6	0.9	1.1	89.7	93.8
256	Frozen prefabricates	0	0	1	0.0	0.0	0.0	96.8	90.2
26-28	Products of other branches	594	1 586	6 551	2.0	1.8	1.4		
26	Feeds and utilized products	228	537	2 024	0.8	0.6	0.4		
261	Mix-feeds	197	460	1 615	0.7	0.5	0.3	35.7	36.8
262	Utilized animal products	30	75	406	0.1	0.1	0.1	62.9	58.9
27	Typographical products	180	493	2 456	0.6	0.6	0.5		
271	Goods of printing	180	493	2 456	0.6	0.6	0.5	20.0	19.4
28	Other industrial products	186	556	2 071	0.6	0.6	0.4		
281	Musical instruments and sound recorders	13	61	226	0.0	0.1	0.0	76.1	79.9
282.283	Dolls and other toys	31	83	268	0.1	0.1	0.1	16.1	24.4
284	Abrasive materials	21	54	273	0.1	0.1	0.1	93.5	95.0
288	Others	118	353	1 252	0.4	0.4	0.3	13.6	26.9

Source : Polish Ministry of Industry and Trade (Promasz).

Table 2.2. **Employment, energy use, productivity and profitability**

Productivity is related to value added
Profitability is related to total production costs

Class.	Product	Value Added 10⁹ zl.	Employment (1990)			Energy use (1990)			Profit before tax [1991(I-VI)]		Net profit [1991(I-VI)]	
			1000	Productivity 10⁹ zl. per person	relativ. %	10¹² J.	Productivity zl. per 10⁶ J.	relativ. %	10⁹ zl.	Profita-bility %	10⁹ zl.	Profita-bility %
01-28	Total industry	165 135	3 661.5	45.1	100.0	4 906 122	34	100.0	23 671	9.1	-637	-0.2
01-03	Energy	35 702	569.3	62.7	139.0	2 993 617	12	35.4				
01	Coal and briquets	15 870	395.8	40.1	88.9	124 555	127	378.5	121	0.5	-1746	-7.1
011	Hard coal	13 282	363.8	36.5	81.0	112 530	118	350.7	-903	-4.1	-2197	-9.9
014	Brown coal	2 332	27.9	83.6	185.3	12 024	194	576.1	935	48.1	410	21.1
02	Fuel	8 713	53.2	163.8	363.2	1 258 778	7	20.6	585	2.8	-782	-3.7
021	Coke	1 537	11.7	131.3	291.2	458 894	3	9.9	303	8.6	-34	-1.0
022	Gas	4 090	17.8	229.8	509.4	45 999	89	264.2	198	16.0	37	3.0
023	Crude petroleum and natural gas	53	7.5	7.1	15.7	1666	32	94.9	-1255	-21.5	-1337	-22.9
024	Liquid fuel and other petroleum products	5 607	16.2	346.1	767.4	752 219	7	22.1	1 339	12.9	552	5.3
03	Power	11 118	120.3	92.4	204.9	1 610 284	7	20.5	343	1.5	-1535	-6.6
031	Power production	8 006	61.1	131.0	290.6	1 561 721	5	15.2	750	4.8	-291	-1.9
033	Power distribution	3 006	56.9	52.8	117.1	48 563	62	183.9	-429	-5.6	-1256	-16.4
04-05	Metallurgy	37 431	183.5	204.0	452.3	651 719	57	170.6				
04	Iron and steel	9164	129.4	70.8	157.0	600 705	15	45.3	1 919	9.4	101	0.5
042	Iron products	8784	124.5	70.6	156.4	600 340	15	43.5	1 778	9.0	21	0.1
048	Manufacturing of scraps	322	2.9	111.1	246.4	349	924	2 743.8	145	26.9	84	15.7

Table 2.2. (continued)

Class.	Product	Value Added 10⁹ zl.	Employment (1990) 1000	Productivity 10⁹ zl. per person	relativ. %	Energy use (1990) 10¹² J.	Productivity zl. per 10⁶ J.	relativ. %	Profit before tax [1991(I-VI)] 10⁹ zl.	Profitability %	Net profit [1991(I-VI)] 10⁹ zl.	Profitability %
05	Non-ferrous products	5 487	54.1	101.4	224.9	51 015	108	319.6	2 039	16.9	642	5.3
051	Ores - non copper	236	3.0	78.8	174.6	5 190	46	135.3	79	30.1	14	5.5
052	Copper ores	1 712	18.3	93.6	207.5	12 181	141	417.6	652	25.1	137	5.3
053	Non-copper products	908	15.8	57.4	127.4	9 786	93	275.5	268	9.8	38	1.4
054	Copper products	2 538	16.2	156.7	347.4	23 665	107	318.7	986	15.4	424	6.6
058	Manufacturing of scraps	90	0.6	150.4	333.5	194	466	1 385.6	55	59.9	30	32.6
06-11	Engineering	34 342	1 130.3	30.4	67.4	178 302	193	572.2				
06	Metal products	6 775	222.5	30.4	67.5	35 374	192	569.0	1 200	12.7	283	3.0
061	Foundry products	1 188	42.5	27.9	62.0	13 886	86	254.1	141	7.2	-87	-4.5
062	Metal structures	661	15.7	42.1	93.3	2 170	304	904.3	159	16.0	62	6.3
063	Bearings	420	14.3	29.4	65.1	3 419	123	364.9	89	17.6	-4	-0.7
064	Metal tools	349	14.7	23.8	52.7	1 210	289	857.5	59	13.8	20	4.6
065	Metal goods for industrial use	1 475	47.4	31.1	69.0	6 829	216	641.6	374	16.4	140	6.2
067	Metal goods for household	1 899	61.7	30.8	68.2	7 314	260	771.2	371	11.9	155	5.0
068	Services (repairing etc)	153	6.0	25.5	56.4	546	280	830.8	6	4.1	-4	-2.4
07-08	Machinery	11 868	355.8	33.4	74.0	59 875	198	588.9	2 414	16.6	483	3.3
071	Boilers, turbines	1 747	51.0	34.3	75.9	9 260	189	560.5	354	17.5	95	4.7
072	For mining industry	1 200	30.3	39.6	87.8	7 250	166	491.7	403	22.1	165	9.1
073	For metallurgy	451	11.4	39.6	87.7	4 614	98	290.5	142	27.4	21	4.1
074	Metal-working machinery	730	26.2	27.9	61.8	4 501	162	481.8	176	18.3	68	7.0
075	For chemistry	542	12.1	44.8	99.3	3 504	155	459.5	262	55.5	96	20.4
076	For building materials	151	4.9	30.8	68.3	480	314	932.7	33	19.7	9	5.6
077	For light industry	173	11.3	15.3	33.9	1 441	120	356.1	-33	-11.5	-55	-19.1
078	For food industry	461	13.3	34.7	76.9	2 131	216	643.1	169	33.2	60	11.7

Table 2.2. (continued)

Class.	Product	Value Added 10⁹ zl.	Employment (1990)			Energy use (1990)			Profit before tax [1991(I-VI)]		Net profit [1991(I-VI)]	
			1000	Productivity		10¹² J.	Productivity		10⁹ zl.	Profitability %	10⁹ zl.	Profitability %
				10⁹ zl. per person	relativ. %		zl. per 10⁶ J.	relativ. %				
079	For wood and paper industry	391	12.2	32.1	71.1	1 412	277	823.0	73	17.7	26	6.3
081	For construction	879	37.5	23.4	51.9	9 130	96	285.9	-97	-5.9	-174	-10.7
082	For agriculture	480	30.8	15.6	34.5	5 674	85	251.2	-234	-18.3	-347	-27.1
084	For trade and storage	273	6.9	39.5	87.7	879	310	922.2	79	23.4	50	14.9
085	Cranes and other transport equipt.	503	15.8	31.8	70.6	2 084	241	717.1	145	20.2	58	8.1
086	Compressors, air conditioning machines	238	5.5	43.2	95.9	783	304	902.0	96	33.3	50	17.4
087	Pumps, ventilators, other general purpose devices	806	20.3	39.7	88.0	3 014	267	794.5	310	37.2	121	14.5
088	Services (repairing etc)	1 797	52.5	34.2	75.9	3 718	483	1 436.0	444	23.4	192	10.1
09	Precision instruments	1 640	63.9	25.7	56.9	5 131	320	949.5	263	12.8	42	2.0
091	Controlling equipment	534	16.0	33.4	74.1	1 008	530	1 575.0	190	31.7	77	12.8
092	Computers and data processing machines	167	9.6	17.4	38.6	650	257	762.7	-71	-15.7	-79	-17.6
094	Measuring equipment	444	17.9	24.8	55.0	1 920	231	687.7	122	21.4	65	11.5
095	Optical goods	77	5.0	15.4	34.2	827	93	276.9	-3	-2.1	-23	-18.5
096	Electronic measuring equipment	16	1.2	13.3	29.5	41	386	1 147.6	-1	-2.0	-1	-5.0
097	Medical equipment	174	7.0	24.8	55.1	638	273	810.2	14	6.6	-3	-1.2
098	Services	71	2.3	30.7	68.1	47	1 505	4 471.4	11	18.1	5	8.7
10	Transport equipment	8 158	284.2	28.7	63.6	53 435	153	453.6	437	2.9	-1 057	-6.9
101	For railroad	832	19.6	42.4	94.1	6 431	129	384.2	432	27.8	185	11.9
102	Motor vehicles	2 708	97.9	27.7	61.3	17 219	157	467.3	-155	-2.7	-442	-7.6
103	Tractors (agricultural)	392	18.2	21.5	47.7	4 868	80	239.0	-348	-26.3	-444	-33.5
104	Motor cycles and bicycles	312	8.4	37.2	82.5	928	337	1 000.6	33	7.0	20	4.2
105	Ships	517	33.9	15.2	33.8	5 192	100	295.8	-192	-9.8	-595	-30.5

171

Table 2.2. (continued)

Class.	Product	Value Added 10⁹ zl.	Employment (1990) 1000	Employment (1990) Productivity 10⁹ zl. per person	Employment (1990) Productivity relativ. %	Energy use (1990) 10¹² J.	Energy use (1990) Productivity zl. per 10⁹J.	Energy use (1990) Productivity relativ. %	Profit before tax [1991(I-VI)] 10⁹ zl.	Profit before tax [1991(I-VI)] Profitability %	Net profit [1991(I-VI)] 10⁹ zl.	Net profit [1991(I-VI)] Profitability %
106	Aircraft	---	25.6	---	---	6 317	---	---	---	---	---	---
107	Containers	24	0.5	49.0	108.5	146	168	498.3	1	0.8	1	0.7
108	Services (repairing etc)	2 459	70.5	34.9	77.3	12 329	199	592.5	579	17.9	213	6.6
11	Electrical and electronics apparatus	5 900	203.9	28.9	64.2	24 487	241	715.9	745	7.6	-195	-2.0
111	Motors, transformers	1 495	37.5	39.9	88.4	5 701	262	779.0	629	34.6	284	15.6
112	Cables and wires	822	10.8	76.1	168.8	2 535	324	963.7	313	13.7	142	6.2
113	Electricity supply	1 221	37.1	32.9	73.0	6 312	194	574.9	315	17.3	114	6.3
115	Electronics	1 470	86.9	16.9	37.5	8 785	167	497.2	-637	-19.6	-786	24.2
116	Telecommunication apparatus and equipt.	309	14.0	22.0	48.9	825	374	1 111.1	62	13.4	23	4.9
118	Services (repairing etc)	306	7.2	42.5	94.2	329	929	2 760.9	0	0.0	0	0.0
12-13	Chemicals	14 660	260.7	56.2	124.7	474 378	31	91.8	4158	16.8	1 034	4.2
121	Chemical crudes excl. sulphur	-	4.2	-	-	4 576	-	-	-	-	-	-
122	Inorganic products	904	11.8	76.6	169.9	61 036	15	44.0	254	16.3	78	5.0
123	Fertilizers	2 150	24.5	87.7	194.6	196 739	11	32.5	303	6.1	-244	-4.9
124	Organic products	1 222	23.7	51.6	114.3	33 678	36	107.8	347	11.3	65	2.1
126	Plastics	494	8.9	55.5	123.2	27 287	18	53.8	163	14.6	41	3.6
127	Chemical fibres	671	21.4	31.4	69.6	32 818	20	60.8	12	0.8	-119	-7.8
128	Chemicals for industry	134	2.7	49.5	109.8	1 007	133	394.5	30	10.9	11	4.0
131	Paints	758	7.7	98.4	218.2	1 969	385	1 143.2	316	23.5	112	8.3
132	Soaps, detergents, cosmetics	1 006	18.4	54.7	121.2	5 577	180	536.0	273	17.4	122	7.8
133	Specialized chemicals	495	8.3	59.6	132.3	2 795	177	526.2	231	37.2	76	12.3
134	Pharmaceuticals	1 444	20.9	69.1	153.2	8 622	167	497.6	873	44.6	430	22.0

Table 2.2.   (continued)

Class.	Product	Value Added 10⁹ zl.	Employment (1990) 1000	Productivity 10⁹ zl. per person	relativ. %	Energy use (1990) 10¹² J	Productivity zl. per 10⁶ J	relativ. %	Profit before tax [1991(I-VI)] 10⁹ zl.	Profita-bility %	Net profit [1991(I-VI)] 10⁹ zl.	Profita-bility %
135	Herbal products	226	3.7	61.1	135.5	614	368	1 094.5	116	48.2	53	21.9
136	Plastic products	1 934	46.5	41.6	92.2	14 298	135	401.9	578	20.0	264	9.2
137	Rubber products	1 067	31.1	34.3	76.1	16 941	63	187.1	170	9.9	-1	-0.1
138	Sulphur	-	13.0	-	-	65 670	-	-	-	-	-	-
14-16	Minerals	7 133	205.0	34.8	77.2	180 225	40	117.6				
14	Building materials	5 091	136.1	37.4	82.9	138 336	37	109.3	1 039	15.0	-171	-2.5
141	Mineral crudes, non-metallic	1 008	27.7	36.4	80.7	6 777	149	441.7	229	19.0	-44	-3.7
142	Cement	1 295	18.6	69.6	154.3	73 627	18	52.2	339	21.1	42	2.6
143	Lime and gypsum products	170	5.2	32.7	72.5	11 060	15	45.7	51	14.3	14	4.0
144	Bricks and tiles, made of clay	461	22.1	20.9	46.3	22 679	20	60.4	-5	-0.7	-108	-16.2
145	Concrete products	1 139	37.3	30.5	67.7	14 845	77	227.9	179	9.7	-148	-8.0
146	Insulation materials	299	6.3	47.5	105.3	4 412	68	201.5	102	17.4	23	3.9
147	Refractory materials	400	7.2	55.5	123.1	4 816	83	246.6	142	23.6	50	8.2
148	Others	-	0.6	-	-	120	-	-	-		-	
15	Glass	1 405	46.0	30.5	67.7	32 212	44	129.6	276	13.6	83	4.1
151	For building	307	7.6	40.5	89.7	9 150	34	99.8	88	17.3	26	5.1
152	For industry and household	573	27.1	21.1	46.8	10 127	57	168.0	30	3.7	-8	-1.0
154	Bottles and other containers	472	9.7	48.7	107.9	12 936	36	108.4	158	22.5	66	9.3
16	Ceramic products	637	22.9	27.8	61.7	9 676	66	195.5	106	14.5	-8	-1.1
161	Porcelain and similar	349	14.7	23.7	52.6	5 274	66	196.6	21	4.8	-46	-10.7
162	Stonewares	50	2.5	19.8	44.0	1 286	39	114.6	5	7.8	-4	-6.9
163	Faience goods	234	5.3	44.1	97.8	3 116	75	222.8	80	34.1	42	17.9

Table 2.2. (continued)

Class.	Product	Value Added 10⁹ zl.	Employment (1990)			Energy use (1990)			Profit before tax [1991(I-VI)]		Net profit [1991(I-VI)]	
			1000	Productivity		10¹² J.	Productivity		10⁹ zl.	Profita-bility %	10⁹ zl.	Profita-bility %
				10⁹ zl. per person	relativ. %		zl. per 10⁶ J.	relativ. %				
17-18	Wood and paper products	7 070	217.3	32.5	72.1	135 280	52	155.3				
17	Wood products	5 062	176.0	28.8	63.8	49 398	102	304.5	532	6.4	108	1.3
171	Sawnwood	1 336	31.4	42.6	94.4	9 414	142	421.7	225	10.1	93	4.2
172	Boards, veneers and plywood	574	15.1	38.0	84.3	19 077	30	89.5	159	12.3	77	6.0
173	Materials for building	295	13.0	22.7	50.4	2 665	111	329.2	44	6.2	-15	-2.1
174	Furnitures	2 195	86.2	25.5	56.5	17 269	127	377.6	119	3.2	-24	-0.6
176	Matches	54	1.5	36.2	80.2	382	142	422.4	4	6.6	0	-0.7
177	Others	81	4.6	17.7	39.3	547	149	442.5	-11	-9.0	-14	-10.8
18	Paper products	2 008	41.4	48.5	107.6	85 882	23	69.5	271	7.1	54	1.4
181	Cellulose, paper and paperboards	1 523	27.3	55.8	123.7	81 291	19	55.7	164	5.6	23	0.8
182	Goods made of paper	482	13.6	35.5	78.6	4 591	105	312.0	107	12.0	30	3.4
19-22	Light industry	10 757	559.2	19.2	42.7	79 891	135	400.0				
19-20	Textiles	5 356	249.0	21.5	47.7	66 787	80	238.3	66	0.7	-527	-5.7
191	Cotton woven fabrics (or similar)	1 231	59.0	20.9	46.2	25 819	48	141.6	-205	-8.6	-305	-12.7
192	Wool woven fabrics (or similar)	707	42.4	16.7	37.0	12 348	57	170.1	-97	-6.5	-171	-11.5
193	Fabrics made of bast fibres	430	21.3	20.2	44.8	10 563	41	121.1	7	0.9	-59	-7.7
194	Silk textiles	263	10.0	26.3	58.4	3 637	72	215.2	14	3.1	-3	-0.7
195	Tapestry	618	17.8	34.7	77.0	3 207	193	572.3	193	26.7	78	10.9
196	Cordage, rope and twine	99	3.5	28.2	62.6	384	257	763.5	20	14.7	5	3.7
201	Knittings and stockings	1 461	77.0	19.0	42.1	8 947	163	485.1	1	0.0	-110	-4.6
202	Goods made of felt	274	6.3	43.5	96.6	1 028	267	792.6	118	20.4	49	8.4
206	Non-weaved textiles	43	2.4	17.9	39.7	545	79	234.3	8	5.2	0	0.1
207	Others	96	3.6	26.6	59.1	308	311	923.7	8	5.3	-11	-7.5

174

Table 2.2. (continued)

Class.	Product	Value Added [10⁹ zl.]	Employment (1990)			Energy use (1990)			Profit before tax [1991(I-VI)]		Net profit [1991(I-VI)]	
			1000	Productivity 10⁹ zl. per person	relativ. %	10¹² J.	Productivity zl. per 10⁶ J.	relativ. %	10⁹ zl.	Profitability %	10⁹ zl.	Profitability %
21	Wearing apparels	3 482	193.5	18.0	39.9	4 035	863	2 563.8	365	9.1	170	4.2
211	Clothes and underwear	2 436	137.1	17.8	39.4	3 228	755	2 241.9	317	9.9	144	4.5
218	Bed linen, articles	-	31.7	-	-	806	-	-	-	-	-	-
22	Leather products	1 919	116.7	16.4	36.5	9 069	212	628.7	-19	-0.5	-123	-3.2
221	Leathers	308	11.2	27.5	61.0	3 906	79	234.3	6	0.8	-26	-3.1
222	Footwear	1 158	79.4	14.6	32.3	4 236	273	812.0	-29	-1.2	-88	-3.6
223	Furs	133	8.8	15.2	33.6	476	280	833.3	-11	-3.9	-17	-6.3
227	Other leather goods	-	10.8	-	-	452	-	-	-	-	-	-
23-25	Food products	38 113	437.9	87.0	193.0	199 943	191	566.3	5 904	14.5	2 191	5.4
231	Meat and meat products	3 628	82.5	44.0	97.5	19 775	183	545.0	1 381	13.6	671	6.6
233	Poultry, eggs and products	732	19.8	37.0	82.0	5 472	134	397.7	225	10.5	105	4.9
234	Fish and products	1 250	26.1	47.9	106.2	15 748	79	235.8	-17	-0.8	-80	-3.8
235	Milk and diary products	2 040	77.9	26.2	58.1	39 350	52	154.0	-47	-0.6	-131	-1.7
241	Flour, cereal. macaroni	1 007	22.9	44.0	97.5	3 602	279	830.2	-138	-6.2	-291	-13.1
242	Bread and baker's wares	445	11.3	39.3	87.2	2 233	199	591.3	94	11.5	41	5.0
243	Sugar	2 837	27.2	104.3	231.3	66 880	42	126.0	224	8.0	10	0.4
244	Alcoholic beverages	10 707	8.3	1 290.0	2 860.3	6 326	1 692	5 028.4	1 303	70.6	569	30.8
245	Potatoes and products	521	6.0	86.8	192.5	5 025	104	308.0	39	9.5	14	3.3
246	Fruits, vegetables and products	2 080	40.8	51.0	113.0	10 881	191	567.8	-27	-1.1	-82	-3.3
247	Wine and honey	652	5.4	120.8	267.8	1 458	447	1 328.5	114	21.2	61	11.4
248	Beer	2 982	14.4	207.1	459.2	9 531	313	929.5	786	65.3	345	28.6
249	Vegetable oils	471	5.6	84.1	186.5	5 300	89	264.0	134	13.9	56	5.8
251	Cakes, chocolates and sweets	1 584	27.9	56.8	125.9	3 126	507	1 505.4	610	29.3	309	14.9
252	Food concentrates	327	6.0	54.6	121.0	1 290	254	753.8	136	20.1	71	10.5

175

Table 2.2. (continued)

Class.	Product	Value Added 10⁹ zl.	Employment (1990)			Energy use (1990)			Profit before tax [1991(I-VI)]		Net profit [1991(I-VI)]	
			1000	Productivity 10⁹ zl. per person	relativ. %	10¹²J.	Productivity zl. per 10⁶J.	relativ. %	10⁹ zl.	Profita-bility %	10⁹ zl.	Profita-bility %
253	Soft drinks	99	1.0	98.6	218.6	144	686	2 037.6	23	45.4	21	41.3
254	Other food	-	3.6	-	-	588	-	-	-	-	-	-
255	Tobacco, cigarettes	3 125	10.9	286.7	635.6	1 791	1 744	5 182.4	932	59.9	472	30.4
256	Frozen prefabricates	485	9.1	53.3	118.1	1 404	345	1 025.5	70	12.0	3	0.4
26-28	Products of other branches	3 240	98.3	33.0	73.1	9 676	335	994.7				
26	Feeds and utilized products	250	6.1	41.1	91.0	3 056	82	243.5	42	5.2	-13	-1.6
261	Mix-feeds	172	4.0	43.1	95.5	1 635	105	313.0	46	6.8	7	1.1
27	Typographical products	1 295	38.0	34.1	75.6	1 894	684	2 032.5	429	29.6	183	12.6
271	Goods of printing	-	35.2	-	-	1 894	-	-				
28	Other industrial products	1 694	54.1	31.3	69.4	4 727	358	1 064.7	438	22.6	146	7.5
281	Musical instruments and sound recorders	90	2.7	33.5	74.3	385	235	698.0	17	13.6	7	5.9
282	Dolls and other toys	76	5.4	14.0	31.1	264	287	853.9	3	2.5	1	0.4
284	Abrasive materials	104	3.1	33.7	74.6	928	112	334.2	24	14.7	7	4.5
288	Others	334	17.5	19.1	42.3	1 077	310	920.9	52	10.8	18	3.8

Source : Polish Ministry of Industry and Trade (Promasz).

Table 2.3. **Industrial exports**

Classification	Product	Exports in total sales (%)						Share of total industrial exports (%)							
		CMEA			Other			CMEA				Other			
		1988	1989	1990	1988	1989	1990	1988	1989	1990	1991*	1988	1989	1990	1991*
01-28	Total industry	7.5	6.6	4.0	11.3	13.0	20.2	100.0	100.0	100.0	100.0	100.0	100.0	100.0	100.0
01-03	Energy	4.2	3.8	1.9	9.3	14.5	14.3	8.7	6.7	8.5	13.8	12.9	12.9	12.5	13.5
01	Coal and briquets	7.1	7.6	4.8	19.8	38.3	38.8	5.8	3.7	5.3	9.8	10.8	9.4	8.5	8.8
011-013	Hard coal	7.7	8.9	5.5	21.5	44.6	44.4	5.8	3.7	5.3	9.8	10.8	9.4	8.5	8.5
014-015	Brown coal	0.2	0.0	0.0	0.0	0.0	1.2	0.0	0.0	0.0	0.0	0.0	0.0	0.0	0.2
02	Fuel	2.7	3.2	1.4	2.9	7.2	9.4	2.3	2.4	2.4	2.2	1.6	2.8	3.3	3.6
021	Coke	13.1	21.5	6.5	4.2	15.1	18.0	2.1	2.3	2.2	2.2	0.4	0.8	1.2	1.6
022	Gas	0.0	0.0	0.0	0.0	0.0	0.0	0.0	0.0	0.0	0.0	0.0	0.0	0.0	0.0
023	Crude petroleum and natural gas	10.0	3.1	1.3	0.4	1.3	0.8	0.1	0.0	0.0	0.0	0.0	0.0	0.0	0.0
024	Liquid fuel and other petroleum products	0.2	0.1	0.2	3.3	7.3	9.3	0.1	0.1	0.2	0.0	1.2	1.9	2.1	2.0
03	Power	1.5	1.2	0.5	1.8	2.8	2.3	0.6	0.6	0.8	1.8	0.5	0.7	0.7	1.1
04-05	Metallurgy	2.3	1.9	0.6	16.6	18.1	27.0	3.4	3.3	2.0	4.4	16.2	16.0	19.7	22.9
04	Iron and steel	3.2	2.6	0.9	10.0	12.9	22.0	2.7	2.7	2.0	0.6	5.6	6.9	9.7	12.2
041	Ores	0.0	0.2	0.0	20.5	25.7	21.8	0.0	0.0	0.0	0.0	0.4	0.5	0.4	0.1
042	Pig iron and ferroalloys	0.0	0.0	0.0	12.7	22.0	28.9	0.0	0.0	0.0	0.2	0.4	0.6	0.8	0.4
043	Crude steel	0.0	0.0	0.0	0.0	33.0	31.2	0.0	0.0	0.0	0.0	0.0	0.5	0.3	0.0
044	Semi-finished hot rolled products	0.0	0.0	0.0	0.3	0.2	36.0	0.0	0.0	0.0	0.0	0.0	0.0	1.3	1.2
045	Hot rolled finished products	6.1	4.8	1.3	14.6	17.0	24.2	2.3	2.3	1.4	0.2	3.7	4.1	5.3	9.1
046	Pipes	1.6	1.6	1.0	1.5	1.3	3.1	0.1	0.2	0.2	0.0	0.1	0.1	0.1	0.2
047	Cold rolled products	1.7	0.8	0.8	6.0	5.1	7.3	0.2	0.2	0.3	0.1	0.6	0.5	0.5	0.4
048	Forging products	0.4	0.3	0.1	5.6	6.9	13.3	0.0	0.0	0.0	0.0	0.2	0.2	0.3	0.5

Table 2.3. (continued)

Classifi-cation	Product	Exports in total sales (%)						Share of total industrial exports (%)							
		CMEA			Other			CMEA				Other			
		1988	1989	1990	1988	1989	1990	1988	1989	1990	1991*	1988	1989	1990	1991*
05	Non-ferrous products	1.1	0.9	0.1	25.4	26.0	34.6	0.7	0.6	0.1	3.8	10.6	9.2	10.0	10.7
051	Ores	0.0	0.0	0.0	9.9	2.6	6.6	0.0	0.0	0.0	0.0	0.9	0.1	0.4	0.3
052	Scraps	0.0	0.0	0.0	39.1	40.7	59.6	0.0	0.0	0.0	0.0	0.2	0.1	0.2	0.1
053	Metallurgical products	0.5	0.3	0.1	48.1	46.2	54.2	0.1	0.1	0.1	1.4	8.0	7.1	7.6	8.7
054	Metal ceramics products	3.4	1.7	1.1	3.1	2.8	4.7	0.0	0.0	0.0	0.0	0.0	0.0	0.0	0.0
055	Rolled products	3.5	2.3	0.1	11.9	14.6	20.8	0.4	0.4	0.4	2.2	0.9	1.1	1.0	0.7
056	Extruded and drawned products	3.3	1.7	0.1	16.4	18.9	34.5	0.2	0.1	0.1	0.1	0.5	0.6	0.7	0.8
057	Forging products	0.0	0.0	0.0	0.0	0.0	0.0	0.0	0.0	0.0	0.0	0.0	0.0	0.0	0.0
058	Others	0.3	0.3	0.5	1.1	2.1	0.4	0.0	0.0	0.0	0.0	0.0	0.1	0.0	0.0
06-11	Engineering	21.4	20.4	13.3	12.8	15.8	24.0	67.8	72.5	71.7	50.1	27.0	28.4	25.8	22.5
06	Metal products	6.3	5.8	3.4	8.4	11.2	19.4	3.9	4.1	3.8	2.0	3.4	4.0	4.3	4.6
061	Foundry products	3.9	3.6	2.2	5.6	8.2	12.2	0.6	0.6	0.7	0.3	0.6	0.7	0.7	0.8
062	Metal structures	12.3	14.5	5.3	9.1	15.3	28.0	0.9	1.2	0.9	0.5	0.4	0.6	0.9	0.9
063	Bearings	12.8	10.6	6.8	18.4	25.6	39.6	0.4	0.5	0.5	0.2	0.4	0.6	0.6	0.5
064	Metal tools	16.4	16.6	10.3	17.9	20.3	26.9	0.7	0.8	0.7	0.1	0.5	0.5	0.4	0.5
065	Metal goods for industrial use	2.1	1.6	0.9	5.1	7.3	13.3	0.4	0.3	0.0	0.1	0.6	0.7	0.8	0.5
067	Metal goods for household	6.4	4.6	3.8	10.2	10.5	22.2	0.8	0.7	0.0	0.7	0.8	0.9	1.0	1.0
07-08	Machinery	28.2	28.9	18.4	14.0	16.4	28.4	25.6	27.5	27.0	12.3	8.5	7.9	8.3	7.1
071	Boilers, turbines, engines	18.3	18.0	12.4	26.6	26.0	36.9	3.0	3.4	3.3	1.6	2.9	2.5	2.0	2.0
072	For mining industry	23.3	30.2	16.2	9.7	9.3	16.5	3.1	3.9	3.4	1.0	0.9	0.6	0.7	0.4
073	For metalurgy and foundry	105.4	96.2	38.7	14.1	17.0	19.6	2.0	1.9	1.7	1.4	0.2	0.2	0.2	0.3
074	Metal-working machinery	33.5	37.0	21.0	20.3	25.4	35.5	2.1	2.7	2.1	0.3	0.8	0.9	0.7	0.8
075	For chemistry	100.6	96.1	57.5	65.1	62.1	83.1	2.0	2.0	2.3	1.3	0.9	0.6	0.7	0.8
076	For building materials	46.6	56.2	39.0	16.1	26.1	46.3	0.5	0.7	0.7	0.2	0.1	0.2	0.2	0.2
077	For light industry	38.1	43.5	46.1	16.6	17.4	21.9	0.9	1.2	1.4	0.4	0.3	0.2	0.1	0.1
078	For food industry	52.9	49.3	35.7	13.0	11.6	19.3	1.5	1.6	1.8	0.2	0.2	0.2	0.2	0.2

Table 2.3. (continued)

Classifi-cation	Product	Exports in total sales (%)						Share of total industrial exports (%)							
		CMEA			Other			CMEA				Other			
		1988	1989	1990	1988	1989	1990	1988	1989	1990	1991*	1988	1989	1990	1991*
079	For wood and paper industry	53.4	47.4	29.0	24.1	24.4	43.8	1.9	1.9	1.8	0.9	0.6	0.5	0.5	0.5
081	For building	41.7	36.2	16.8	18.0	26.1	51.1	2.9	2.7	2.2	0.7	0.8	1.0	1.4	0.6
082	For agriculture	15.8	10.2	6.5	3.6	4.4	10.3	1.6	1.2	1.0	0.4	0.2	0.3	0.3	0.3
084	For trade and storage	34.2	16.3	21.6	14.4	6.4	20.1	0.6	0.9	1.5	0.8	0.2	0.2	0.3	0.3
085	Cranes and other transport equipment	15.3	30.8	26.1	2.5	7.7	14.1	1.8	1.8	2.2	1.4	0.2	0.2	0.2	0.2
087	Pumps, ventilators, other purpose devices general	17.6	16.3	7.6	3.8	6.5	22.4	1.7	1.7	1.4	1.8	0.2	0.3	0.8	0.5
09	Precision instruments	47.6	58.5	63.4	6.3	7.3	14.2	8.4	10.7	14.8	4.4	0.7	0.7	0.7	0.8
091	Controlling equipment	31.8	36.9	24.3	9.0	10.0	1.5	0.9	1.1	1.3	0.5	0.2	0.2	0.2	0.3
092	Computers and data processing mach.	68.4	93.8	123.0	1.9	1.8	8.9	4.5	6.1	8.4	2.6	0.1	0.1	0.1	0.1
093	Office and calculation equipment	22.5	22.8	23.7	14.5	10.2	24.0	0.0	0.2	0.2	0.0	0.1	0.0	0.0	0.0
094	Measuring equipment	40.7	47.1	49.9	9.3	11.6	19.9	1.9	2.3	3.2	0.9	2.9	0.3	0.3	0.3
095.096	Optical goods	16.7	19.8	30.8	4.7	7.9	10.5	0.2	0.2	0.4	0.1	0.0	0.0	0.0	0.0
097	Medical equipment	32.6	43.8	54.4	10.4	10.5	13.4	0.5	0.8	1.3	0.3	0.1	0.1	0.1	0.1
10	Transport equipment	15.2	15.0	7.9	13.3	17.2	28.8	12.0	13.3	10.8	16.6	7.0	7.7	7.8	5.7
101	For railroad	28.0	26.3	3.1	6.0	15.1	53.3	2.2	2.0	0.7	6.0	0.3	0.6	2.4	0.7
102	Motor vehicles	8.5	7.6	3.1	12.0	10.2	18.4	3.8	3.9	2.4	4.5	3.5	2.7	2.8	0.8
103	Tractors (agricultural)	5.3	4.3	4.6	6.4	13.3	16.4	0.4	0.3	0.5	0.6	0.4	0.5	0.3	0.2
104	Motor cycles and bicycles	2.1	1.3	0.6	9.3	8.5	18.5	0.1	0.0	0.0	0.0	0.2	0.2	0.2	0.2
105	Ships	38.6	41.7	32.5	29.4	49.3	54.7	4.5	5.4	5.2	2.7	2.3	3.2	1.8	3.5
106	Aircraft	29.2	37.2	38.0	11.7	21.2	25.9	1.1	1.6	1.9	2.7	0.3	0.5	0.3	0.2
107	Containers	0.0	0.0	0.0	36.2	35.4	60.0	0.0	0.0	0.0	0.0	0.1	0.1	0.1	0.1
11	Electrical and electronic apparatus	12.2	9.8	7.1	8.2	13.1	16.7	8.3	8.2	8.6	4.4	3.7	5.5	4.0	3.8

Table 2.3. (continued)

Classification	Product	Exports in Total Sales (%)						Share of Total Industrial Exports (%)							
		CMEA			Other			CMEA				Other			
		1988	1989	1990	1988	1989	1990	1988	1989	1990	1991*	1988	1989	1990	1991*
111-113	Electrical machines and apparatus	12.5	9.7	6.0	10.0	18.0	19.6	4.6	4.4	4.5	3.4	2.4	4.1	2.9	3.0
111	Motors. transformers	21.7	20.2	11.8	7.1	10.0	15.6	2.7	2.7	2.8	2.8	0.6	0.7	0.8	0.6
112	Cables and wires	0.3	0.2	0.1	20.4	38.7	32.2	0.0	0.0	0.0	0.4	1.4	3.0	1.7	1.8
113	Electricity supply	13.7	9.9	6.6	4.3	4.8	9.9	1.8	1.6	1.6	0.2	0.4	0.4	0.5	0.6
115	Electronics and telecommunication	11.8	9.9	11.6	6.1	7.4	15.8	3.7	1.2	4.2	1.0	1.3	0.2	1.1	0.8
12-13	Chemicals	7.7	6.9	4.8	14.4	16.8	27.8	10.6	10.3	12.1	17.8	13.1	12.6	13.9	15.4
121	Sulphur salt and other crude	21.0	16.4	8.9	55.9	57.5	66.9	0.1	1.6	1.6	5.4	3.1	2.8	2.4	2.8
122	Inorganic products	1.7	0.9	0.1	30.6	37.9	46.2	0.1	0.1	0.0	1.0	1.7	1.8	2.1	1.9
123	Fertilizers	0.0	0.0	0.0	6.7	10.1	4.4	0.0	0.0	0.0	0.0	0.5	0.5	0.2	2.4
124	Organic products	3.5	3.1	0.8	24.7	31.9	51.6	0.7	0.6	0.3	0.8	3.7	3.3	3.3	3.9
126	Plastics	0.3	0.0	0.0	24.9	25.8	35.4	0.0	0.0	0.0	0.1	1.8	1.5	2.0	2.4
127	Chemical fibres	1.3	1.0	0.7	5.0	6.9	14.0	0.1	0.1	0.1	0.3	0.3	0.3	0.4	0.3
128	Chemicals for industry	0.4	0.3	0.1	11.1	8.2	14.9	0.0	0.0	0.0	0.0	0.3	0.2	0.2	0.2
131	Paints	7.7	4.4	1.4	6.6	9.5	13.1	0.7	0.5	0.2	0.2	0.4	0.5	0.4	0.2
132	Soaps, detergents, cosmetics	8.5	9.9	8.9	1.9	2.4	2.9	0.9	1.1	1.4	0.3	0.1	0.1	0.1	0.1
133	Specialized chemicals	3.9	3.6	3.0	8.6	10.3	5.9	0.3	0.3	0.4	0.1	0.4	0.4	0.2	0.2
134	Pharmaceuticals	44.3	48.1	34.7	4.2	4.9	5.5	5.3	5.4	7.0	8.6	0.3	0.3	0.2	0.2
135	Herbal products	1.8	3.3	0.7	5.4	6.0	10.3	0.0	0.1	0.0	0.0	0.1	0.1	0.1	0.1
136	Plastic products	1.9	2.4	2.3	3.2	2.3	4.6	0.3	0.4	0.7	0.4	0.3	0.2	0.3	0.2
137	Rubber products	2.8	2.0	1.6	6.5	7.9	13.3	0.3	0.3	0.3	0.6	0.5	0.5	0.5	0.6
14-16	Minerals	1.1	0.9	0.5	6.2	7.0	12.2	0.5	0.5	0.5	0.8	2.0	1.9	2.2	2.9
14	Building materials	0.4	0.6	0.2	2.6	3.1	5.4	0.2	0.2	0.1	0.4	0.6	0.6	0.7	0.9
141	Mineral crudes, non-metallic	0.3	0.4	0.2	2.0	2.8	3.8	0.0	0.0	0.0	0.0	0.1	0.1	0.1	0.1

Table 2.3. (continued)

Classifi-cation	Product	Exports in total sales (%) CMEA			Other			Share of total industrial exports (%) CMEA				Other			
		1988	1989	1990	1988	1989	1990	1988	1989	1990	1991*	1988	1989	1990	1991*
142	Cement	0.4	0.5	0.0	8.7	9.2	14.5	0.0	0.0	0.0	0.0	0.4	0.4	0.5	0.6
143	Lime and gypsum products	0.9	0.7	0.7	3.2	2.3	3.9	0.0	0.0	0.0	0.0	0.0	0.0	0.0	0.0
144	Bricks and tiles, made of clay	0.1	0.1	0.1	0.3	0.1	0.5	0.0	0.0	0.0	0.0	0.0	0.0	0.0	0.0
145	Concrete products	0.4	0.4	0.1	0.1	0.1	2.1	0.0	0.0	0.0	0.0	0.0	0.0	0.1	0.1
146	Insulation materials	0.6	2.4	0.5	0.2	1.7	1.5	0.0	0.1	0.0	0.2	0.0	0.0	0.0	0.0
147	Refractory materials	0.9	0.4	0.5	1.5	1.1	2.2	0.0	0.0	0.0	0.2	0.0	0.0	0.0	0.0
148	Others	0.0	0.0	0.0	1.7	2.2	2.1	0.0	0.0	0.0	0.0	0.0	0.0	0.0	0.0
15	Glass	3.2	1.7	1.5	16.8	16.5	32.1	0.3	0.2	0.3	0.3	1.1	1.0	1.2	1.7
151	For building	2.5	0.6	0.2	30.2	20.6	37.4	0.0	0.0	0.0	0.1	0.4	0.3	0.3	0.5
152.153	For industry and household	4.4	3.2	2.5	21.9	23.3	38.3	0.2	0.2	0.2	0.2	0.6	0.6	0.6	0.8
154	Bottles and other containers	2.2	0.5	1.0	3.8	5.9	20.0	0.1	0.0	0.1	0.0	0.1	0.1	0.2	0.4
16	Ceramic products	1.9	1.1	0.9	12.8	11.6	22.7	0.1	0.1	0.1	0.0	0.3	0.3	0.3	0.4
161	Porcelain and similar	2.9	2.1	0.8	22.5	23.2	20.9	0.1	0.1	0.1	0.0	0.3	0.3	0.3	0.4
162	Stonewares	1.1	0.4	0.1	4.5	1.2	0.6	0.0	0.0	0.0	0.0	0.0	0.0	0.0	0.0
163	Faience goods	0.8	0.2	0.3	2.1	1.9	9.1	0.0	0.0	0.0	0.0	0.0	0.0	0.0	0.0
17-18	Wood and paper	1.6	0.9	0.5	14.2	12.9	22.8	1.0	0.6	0.6	0.3	5.4	4.7	4.8	5.8
17	Wood products	2.3	1.2	0.8	17.4	15.0	28.5	0.9	0.6	0.5	0.1	4.4	3.7	3.8	4.4
171	Sawnwood	0.1	0.0	0.0	28.7	23.7	31.4	0.0	0.0	0.0	0.0	1.5	1.3	1.1	1.0
172	Boards, veneers and plywood	0.3	0.1	0.2	15.9	13.7	25.6	0.0	0.0	0.0	0.0	0.6	0.5	0.5	0.6
173	Materials for building	0.1	0.0	0.0	1.3	0.7	7.3	0.0	0.0	0.0	0.0	0.0	0.0	0.1	0.1
174	Furnitures	4.5	2.4	1.7	15.4	15.4	32.9	0.8	0.5	0.5	0.0	1.9	1.7	1.9	2.5
175	Packages	0.6	0.4	0.2	14.8	8.6	25.8	0.0	0.0	0.0	0.0	0.1	0.0	0.1	0.0
176	Matches	0.0	0.0	0.0	11.9	9.1	5.4	0.0	0.0	0.0	0.0	0.0	0.0	0.0	0.0
177	Others	2.3	0.9	0.0	25.7	11.4	0.9	0.0	0.0	0.0	0.0	0.3	0.1	0.0	0.1

Table 2.3. (continued)

Classifi-cation	Product	Exports in total sales (%)						Share of total industrial exports (%)							
		CMEA			Other			CMEA				Other			
		1988	1989	1990	1988	1989	1990	1988	1989	1990	1991*	1988	1989	1990	1991*
18	Paper products	0.3	0.2	0.1	7.8	8.4	13.3	0.1	0.0	0.0	0.2	1.0	1.0	1.1	1.4
181	Cellulose, paper and paperboards	0.1	0.1	0.0	15.3	15.7	23.2	0.0	0.0	0.0	0.2	1.0	0.9	1.0	1.4
182	Goods made of paper	0.6	0.3	0.1	0.5	0.4	1.0	0.1	0.0	0.0	0.0	0.0	0.0	0.0	0.0
19-22	Light industry	3.5	2.0	1.3	8.5	7.9	22.1	5.3	3.8	2.3	2.9	8.7	7.4	7.8	6.4
19-20	Textiles	2.3	1.7	1.4	7.7	6.8	14.4	2.0	1.8	1.3	0.4	4.3	3.5	2.8	2.0
191	Cotton woven fabrics (or similar)	2.2	1.9	1.7	4.8	4.2	13.4	0.6	0.6	0.5	0.1	0.8	0.7	0.7	0.3
192	Wool woven fabrics (or similar)	1.2	0.5	0.4	8.4	7.2	16.5	0.2	0.1	0.1	0.2	0.9	0.7	0.5	0.3
193	Fabrics made of bast fibres	2.9	2.1	0.3	21.7	16.4	35.2	0.1	0.1	0.0	0.0	0.5	0.4	0.2	0.2
194	Silk textiles	1.6	0.8	0.7	7.5	7.1	13.5	0.1	0.0	0.0	0.0	0.2	0.2	0.1	0.1
195	Tapestry	2.7	2.2	1.7	12.3	14.5	13.1	0.2	0.2	0.2	0.0	0.5	0.6	0.3	0.2
196	Cordage, rope and twine	0.3	0.4	0.2	2.3	1.4	4.4	0.0	0.0	0.0	0.0	0.0	0.0	0.0	0.0
201.203	Knittings and stockings	4.1	3.1	2.3	8.9	7.6	16.9	0.8	0.8	0.6	0.1	1.2	1.0	0.8	0.8
202	Goods made of felt	0.0	0.0	0.0	4.9	3.3	5.1	0.0	0.0	0.0	0.0	0.1	0.1	0.1	0.1
206	Non-weaved textiles	0.0	0.0	0.0	0.5	0.3	0.3	0.0	0.0	0.0	0.0	0.0	0.0	0.0	0.0
207	Others	0.7	1.2	1.2	1.9	1.4	5.1	0.0	0.0	0.0	0.0	0.0	0.0	0.0	0.0
21	Wearing apparels	4.7	2.4	1.2	12.0	12.8	41.1	1.6	0.9	0.4	1.8	2.7	2.5	2.9	2.8
211	Clothes and underwear	7.1	3.4	1.5	15.7	15.4	52.3	1.5	0.8	0.4	1.8	2.2	1.9	2.5	2.3
218	Bed linen, articles	0.8	0.6	0.6	6.0	8.2	19.6	0.1	0.1	0.1	0.0	0.5	0.6	0.5	0.5
22	Leather products	5.1	2.4	1.2	7.1	6.1	23.8	1.8	1.0	0.5	0.7	1.6	1.3	2.0	1.6
221	Leathers	0.0	0.0	0.0	1.4	1.3	5.5	0.0	0.0	0.0	0.0	0.1	0.1	0.1	0.1
222	Footwear	7.6	3.3	1.0	8.6	7.3	30.6	1.4	0.8	0.3	0.4	1.1	0.9	1.6	1.3
223	Furs	0.6	0.5	4.2	11.6	9.1	27.4	0.0	0.0	0.1	0.3	0.3	0.2	0.2	0.1
227	Other leather goods	7.0	3.7	2.6	6.5	6.4	20.7	0.3	0.2	0.1	0.0	0.2	0.1	0.1	0.1

Table 2.3. (continued)

Classifi-cation	Product	Exports in total sales (%)						Share of total industrial exports (%)							
		CMEA			Other			CMEA				Other			
		1988	1989	1990	1988	1989	1990	1988	1989	1990	1991*	1988	1989	1990	1991*
23-25	Food products	0.8	0.5	0.4	9.0	9.5	14.1	1.9	1.6	1.6	9.8	14.2	15.4	12.6	9.9
231.232	Meat and meat products	0.0	0.0	0.0	11.5	9.9	13.9	0.0	0.0	0.0	b.d.	3.6	3.5	2.8	b.d.
233	Poultry, eggs and products	0.0	0.0	0.0	15.1	22.2	26.6	0.0	0.0	0.0	b.d.	1.0	1.3	0.9	b.d.
234	Fish and products	0.8	0.4	0.1	50.9	52.2	69.0	0.1	0.0	0.0	b.d.	2.4	2.0	1.9	b.d.
235	Milk and diary products	0.1	0.0	0.0	8.8	8.5	13.7	0.0	0.0	0.0	b.d.	1.8	2.0	1.5	b.d.
241	Flour, cereal, macaroni	0.0	0.0	0.5	0.1	0.1	0.1	0.0	0.0	0.0	b.d.	0.0	0.0	0.0	b.d.
242	Bread and baker's wares	2.9	1.4	0.5	0.9	0.6	0.4	0.0	0.0	0.0	b.d.	0.0	0.0	0.0	b.d.
243	Sugar	0.0	0.0	0.2	9.3	11.2	21.9	0.0	0.0	0.1	b.d.	0.8	1.7	1.7	b.d.
244	Alcoholic beverages	0.1	0.3	0.4	1.2	1.9	2.8	0.1	0.2	0.3	b.d.	0.5	0.6	0.4	b.d.
245	Potatoes and products	1.8	1.0	2.8	7.2	7.2	33.5	0.0	0.0	0.1	b.d.	0.1	0.1	0.2	b.d.
246	Fruits, vegetables and products	11.2	6.1	4.4	40.6	36.1	59.0	1.1	0.7	0.6	b.d.	2.6	2.2	1.6	b.d.
247	Wine and honey	0.0	0.0	0.0	0.5	0.6	1.0	0.0	0.0	0.0	b.d.	0.0	0.0	0.0	b.d.
248	Beer	1.0	0.4	0.0	1.3	1.5	2.2	0.1	0.0	0.0	b.d.	0.1	0.1	0.1	b.d.
249	Vegetable oils	0.0	0.0	0.0	7.2	19.4	18.5	0.0	0.0	0.0	b.d.	0.2	0.7	0.4	b.d.
251	Cakes, chocolates and sweets	0.9	0.5	0.2	5.8	4.7	4.8	0.1	0.1	0.0	b.d.	0.4	0.4	0.2	b.d.
252	Food concentrates	6.5	4.5	4.4	1.2	1.2	2.2	0.2	0.2	0.2	b.d.	0.0	0.0	0.0	b.d.
253	Soft drinks	0.0	0.0	0.0	0.4	1.1	0.7	0.0	0.0	0.0	b.d.	0.0	0.0	0.0	b.d.
254	Other food	7.0	6.9	3.0	7.2	12.9	27.0	0.2	0.2	0.1	b.d.	0.1	0.2	0.2	b.d.
255	Tobacco, cigarettes	0.3	0.3	0.3	8.1	9.3	6.2	0.0	0.0	0.1	b.d.	0.5	0.6	0.3	b.d.
256	Frozen prefabricates	0.0	0.0	0.0	0.0	0.0	0.0	0.0	0.0	0.0	b.d.	0.0	0.0	0.0	b.d.
26-28	Products of other branches	2.7	2.6	2.3	2.8	4.4	9.1	0.7	0.7	0.8	0.1	0.5	0.6	0.6	0.3
26	Feeds and utilized products	0.0	0.0	0.0	0.9	1.5	6.2	0.0	0.0	0.0	0.0	0.1	0.1	0.1	0.1
261	Mix-feeds	0.0	0.0	0.0	0.0	0.0	0.0	0.0	0.0	0.0	0.0	0.0	0.0	0.0	0.0
262	Utilized animal products	0.0	0.0	0.0	6.6	10.8	31.2	0.0	0.0	0.0	0.0	0.1	0.1	0.1	0.1

Table 2.3. (continued)

Classifi-cation	Product	Exports in total sales (%)						Share of total industrial exports (%)							
		CMEA			Other			CMEA				Other			
		1988	1989	1990	1988	1989	1990	1988	1989	1990	1991*	1988	1989	1990	1991*
27	Typographical products	2.0	2.0	1.4	0.9	0.9	1.2	0.2	0.2	0.2	0.0	0.0	0.0	0.0	0.0
271	Goods of printing	2.0	2.0	1.4	0.9	0.9	1.2	0.2	0.2	0.2	0.0	0.0	0.0	0.0	0.0
28	Other industrial products	6.7	5.6	5.6	6.9	10.2	21.3	0.6	0.5	0.6	0.1	0.4	0.5	0.5	0.2
281	Musical instruments and sound recorders	9.6	2.9	6.0	22.6	12.9	37.4	0.1	0.0	0.1	0.0	0.1	0.1	0.1	0.0
282,283	Dolls and other toys	12.3	9.0	13.5	15.0	15.6	30.9	0.2	0.1	0.2	0.0	0.1	0.1	0.1	0.1
284	Abrasive materials	1.3	1.4	0.5	15.7	21.5	32.8	0.0	0.0	0.0	0.0	0.1	0.1	0.1	0.0
288	Others	5.9	5.9	5.2	1.4	6.8	15.8	0.3	0.4	0.3	0.0	0.1	0.2	0.2	0.1

*First six months.

Source : Polish Ministry of Industry and Trade (Promasz).

MAIN SALES OUTLETS OF OECD PUBLICATIONS
PRINCIPAUX POINTS DE VENTE DES PUBLICATIONS DE L'OCDE

ARGENTINA – ARGENTINE
Carlos Hirsch S.R.L.
Galería Güemes, Florida 165, 4° Piso
1333 Buenos Aires   Tel. (1) 331.1787 y 331.2391
Telefax: (1) 331.1787

AUSTRALIA – AUSTRALIE
D.A. Book (Aust.) Pty. Ltd.
648 Whitehorse Road, P.O.B 163
Mitcham, Victoria 3132   Tel. (03) 873.4411
Telefax: (03) 873.5679

AUSTRIA – AUTRICHE
Gerold & Co.
Graben 31
Wien I   Tel. (0222) 533.50.14

BELGIUM – BELGIQUE
Jean De Lannoy
Avenue du Roi 202
B-1060 Bruxelles   Tel. (02) 538.51.69/538.08.41
Telefax: (02) 538.08.41

CANADA
Renouf Publishing Company Ltd.
1294 Algoma Road
Ottawa, ON K1B 3W8   Tel. (613) 741.4333
Telefax: (613) 741.5439
Stores:
61 Sparks Street
Ottawa, ON K1P 5R1   Tel. (613) 238.8985
211 Yonge Street
Toronto, ON M5B 1M4   Tel. (416) 363.3171
Les Éditions La Liberté Inc.
3020 Chemin Sainte-Foy
Sainte-Foy, PQ G1X 3V6   Tel. (418) 658.3763
Telefax: (418) 658.3763

Federal Publications
165 University Avenue
Toronto, ON M5H 3B8   Tel. (416) 581.1552
Telefax: (416) 581.1743

CHINA – CHINE
China National Publications Import
Export Corporation (CNPIEC)
16 Gongti E. Road, Chaoyang District
P.O. Box 88 or 50
Beijing 100704 PR   Tel. (01) 506.6688
Telefax: (01) 506.3101

DENMARK – DANEMARK
Munksgaard Export and Subscription Service
35, Nørre Søgade, P.O. Box 2148
DK-1016 København K   Tel. (33) 12.85.70
Telefax: (33) 12.93.87

FINLAND – FINLANDE
Akateeminen Kirjakauppa
Keskuskatu 1, P.O. Box 128
00100 Helsinki   Tel. (358 0) 12141
Telefax: (358 0) 121.4441

FRANCE
OECD/OCDE
Mail Orders/Commandes par correspondance:
2, rue André-Pascal
75775 Paris Cedex 16   Tel. (33-1) 45.24.82.00
Telefax: (33-1) 45.24.85.00   or (33-1) 45.24.81.76
Telex: 640048 OCDE

OECD Bookshop/Librairie de l'OCDE :
33, rue Octave-Feuillet
75016 Paris   Tel. (33-1) 45.24.81.67
(33-1) 45.24.81.81

Documentation Française
29, quai Voltaire
75007 Paris   Tel. 40.15.70.00

Gibert Jeune (Droit-Économie)
6, place Saint-Michel
75006 Paris   Tel. 43.25.91.19

Librairie du Commerce International
10, avenue d'Iéna
75016 Paris   Tel. 40.73.34.60
Librairie Dunod
Université Paris-Dauphine
Place du Maréchal de Lattre de Tassigny
75016 Paris   Tel. 47.27.18.56
Librairie Lavoisier
11, rue Lavoisier
75008 Paris   Tel. 42.65.39.95
Librairie L.G.D.J. - Montchrestien
20, rue Soufflot
75005 Paris   Tel. 46.33.89.85
Librairie des Sciences Politiques
30, rue Saint-Guillaume
75007 Paris   Tel. 45.48.36.02
P.U.F.
49, boulevard Saint-Michel
75005 Paris   Tel. 43.25.83.40
Librairie de l'Université
12a, rue Nazareth
13100 Aix-en-Provence   Tel. (16) 42.26.18.08
Documentation Française
165, rue Garibaldi
69003 Lyon   Tel. (16) 78.63.32.23
Librairie Decitre
29, place Bellecour
69002 Lyon   Tel. (16) 72.40.54.54

GERMANY – ALLEMAGNE
OECD Publications and Information Centre
Schedestrasse 7
D-W 5300 Bonn 1   Tel. (0228) 21.60.45
Telefax: (0228) 26.11.04

GREECE – GRÈCE
Librairie Kauffmann
Mavrokordatou 9
106 78 Athens   Tel. 322.21.60
Telefax: 363.39.67

HONG-KONG
Swindon Book Co. Ltd.
13–15 Lock Road
Kowloon, Hong Kong   Tel. 366.80.31
Telefax: 739.49.75

ICELAND – ISLANDE
Mál Mog Menning
Laugavegi 18, Pósthólf 392
121 Reykjavik   Tel. 162.35.23

INDIA – INDE
Oxford Book and Stationery Co.
Scindia House
New Delhi 110001   Tel.(11) 331.5896/5308
Telefax: (11) 332.5993
17 Park Street
Calcutta 700016   Tel. 240832

INDONESIA – INDONÉSIE
Pdii-Lipi
P.O. Box 269/JKSMG/88
Jakarta 12790   Tel. 583467
Telex: 62 875

IRELAND – IRLANDE
TDC Publishers – Library Suppliers
12 North Frederick Street
Dublin 1   Tel. 74.48.35/74.96.77
Telefax: 74.84.16

ISRAEL
Electronic Publications only
Publications électroniques seulement
Sophist Systems Ltd.
71 Allenby Street
Tel-Aviv 65134   Tel. 3-29.00.21
Telefax: 3-29.92.39

ITALY – ITALIE
Libreria Commissionaria Sansoni
Via Duca di Calabria 1/1
50125 Firenze   Tel. (055) 64.54.15
Telefax: (055) 64.12.57
Via Bartolini 29
20155 Milano   Tel. (02) 36.50.83
Editrice e Libreria Herder
Piazza Montecitorio 120
00186 Roma   Tel. 679.46.28
Telefax: 678.47.51
Libreria Hoepli
Via Hoepli 5
20121 Milano   Tel. (02) 86.54.46
Telefax: (02) 805.28.86
Libreria Scientifica
Dott. Lucio de Biasio 'Aeiou'
Via Coronelli, 6
20146 Milano   Tel. (02) 48.95.45.52
Telefax: (02) 48.95.45.48

JAPAN – JAPON
OECD Publications and Information Centre
Landic Akasaka Building
2-3-4 Akasaka, Minato-ku
Tokyo 107   Tel. (81.3) 3586.2016
Telefax: (81.3) 3584.7929

KOREA – CORÉE
Kyobo Book Centre Co. Ltd.
P.O. Box 1658, Kwang Hwa Moon
Seoul   Tel. 730.78.91
Telefax: 735.00.30

MALAYSIA – MALAISIE
Co-operative Bookshop Ltd.
University of Malaya
P.O. Box 1127, Jalan Pantai Baru
59700 Kuala Lumpur
Malaysia   Tel. 756.5000/756.5425
Telefax: 757.3661

NETHERLANDS – PAYS-BAS
SDU Uitgeverij
Christoffel Plantijnstraat 2
Postbus 20014
2500 EA's-Gravenhage   Tel. (070 3) 78.99.11
Voor bestellingen: Tel. (070 3) 78.98.80
Telefax: (070 3) 47.63.51

NEW ZEALAND
NOUVELLE-ZÉLANDE
Legislation Services
P.O. Box 12418
Thorndon, Wellington   Tel. (04) 496.5652
Telefax: (04) 496.5698

NORWAY – NORVÈGE
Narvesen Info Center – NIC
Bertrand Narvesens vei 2
P.O. Box 6125 Etterstad
0602 Oslo 6   Tel. (02) 57.33.00
Telefax: (02) 68.19.01

PAKISTAN
Mirza Book Agency
65 Shahrah Quaid-E-Azam
Lahore 3   Tel. 66.839
Telex: 44886 UBL PK. Attn: MIRZA BK

PORTUGAL
Livraria Portugal
Rua do Carmo 70-74
Apart. 2681
1117 Lisboa Codex   Tel.: (01) 347.49.82/3/4/5
Telefax: (01) 347.02.64